Order this book online at www.trafford.com/07-2710
or email orders@trafford.com

Most Trafford titles are also available at major online book retailers.

© Copyright 2008 Anthea Lawrence

All rights reserved. No part of this publication may be reproduced, stored in a retrieval system, or transmitted, in any form or by any means, electronic, mechanical, photocopying, recording, or otherwise, without the written prior permission of the author.

Note for Librarians: A cataloguing record for this book is available from Library and Archives Canada at www.collectionscanada.ca/amicus/index-e.html

Printed in Victoria, BC, Canada.

ISBN: 978-1-4251-5986-3

We at Trafford believe that it is the responsibility of us all, as both individuals and corporations, to make choices that are environmentally and socially sound. You, in turn, are supporting this responsible conduct each time you purchase a Trafford book, or make use of our publishing services. To find out how you are helping, please visit www.trafford.com/responsiblepublishing.html

Our mission is to efficiently provide the world's finest, most comprehensive book publishing service, enabling every author to experience success. To find out how to publish your book, your way, and have it available worldwide, visit us online at www.trafford.com/10510

Trafford PUBLISHING www.trafford.com

North America & international
toll-free: 1 888 232 4444 (USA & Canada)
phone: 250 383 6864 ♦ fax: 250 383 6804 ♦ email: info@trafford.com

The United Kingdom & Europe
phone: +44 (0)1865 722 113 ♦ local rate: 0845 230 9601
facsimile: +44 (0)1865 722 868 ♦ email: info.uk@trafford.com

10 9 8 7 6 5 4 3 2 1

Further Control
Anthea Lawrence

The How & Why of Advanced
Gundog Training
(For any variety gundog)

The photograph on the front cover and title page shows Mary Ward with her Flat Coated Retriever, Parsifal Prelude (Nuala, to her friends).
The photograph was taken, and is used, by kind permission of Sharon Rogers Sharon@woodmist.co.uk

Acknowledgements

A special thank you to the following:

For allowing me to use their wonderful photographs;

Richard Ashdown
Nigel Haines
Sharon Rogers
Sonia Skinner

David Tomlinson
Sarah Tunnicliffe
Mary Ward

For help with reading, checking and suggested changes;

Carol Carpenter
Sarah Tunnicliffe

Sonia Skinner
Mary Ward

As always, I could not have completed this book without the experience and inspiration gained from the privilege of working with so many people and dogs. Every person, every dog gives me so much, and so many opportunities to discover how each unique partnership can learn best. Those who know me well will know that I am never happier than when I have a dog training issue to address. I thrive on seeing a problem and finding out the best way to deal with it. A big thank you, therefore, to all those who bring their dogs to me so that I can share them with you and be part of their learning experiences.

Finally: for keeping me sane by being there for me; always being willing to discuss training issues; helping by teaching others the methods I advocate; thanks to my special friend

Mary Ward

(Photograph: Anthea Lawrence)

Mary, showing true dedication to duty as an instructor, on a puppy water training course.

Normally it's the puppies, and not the instructors, which are encouraged to actually enter the water!

Dedication

For my special girl Bebe (Merryway Bebe of Courtridge) who has taught, and given, me so much

Be celebrated her 13th birthday in August 2007. She won her first Open GWT at the age of 22 months and has won numerous other tests from Puppy through to Veteran.

As well as gaining a variety of other places in GWT's she was a member of the MGRC team when they won the Golden Retriever Clubs Inter-Club event in 1997. She has been in numerous demonstrations and has helped me for many years in taking classes and demonstrating exercises. She has also tirelessly retrieved all manner of articles from ponds and streams in the process of teaching puppies to swim and retrieve from water for many years.

Her achievements include: 8 Field Trial awards;
Bronze, Silver and Gold Good Citizen Awards;
The Working Gundog Certificate.

Me and my friend

Bebe
On the day she came to live with us in 1994

Doing one of the things she likes best.

With her 11 puppies born in 1996

On her 13th Birthday 2007, still ready to play with her grand-daughter Gemma.

(Photographs: Anthea Lawrence)

Contents.

Introduction 1-2

Chapter One — 5-14
The Use and Abuse of the Stop Whistle

Chapter Two — 15-30
The Stop Whistle – Training and Exercises

Chapter Three — 32-44
Hunting and Scent

Chapter Four — 45-61
Hunting – Training and Exercises

Chapter Five — 64-70
Double retrieves, Diversions and Distractions

Chapter Six — 73-89
Double retrieves – Training and Exercises

Chapter Seven — 90-107
Diversions and Distractions – Training and Exercises

Chapter Eight — 108-123
Obedience - or obedience?

Chapter Nine — 127-139
Directional commands

Chapter Ten — 140-156
Diagonal directional commands – Training and Exercises

Chapter Eleven — 157-170
Water work

Chapter Twelve — 174-195
Water – Training and Exercises

Chapter Thirteen — 196-214
Common problems – Prevention and Treatment

Chapter Fourteen — 215-233
Have your foundations started to crumble?

Conclusion 234-239

Photographs

'Sit', means sit, no matter what……'	3
The stop whistle	31
Hunting and Dogging-in	62
Dealing with retrieved birds	63
Distractions	71-72
Hand signal positions	124-126
Water experience and work	171-173
Swapping dummies	205-209

Further Control

Introduction

In *'Taking Control'* handlers will have learnt how to teach a young gundog the basics of training which will be required, and remain the same, for ever. These aspects of training form the foundations upon which all subsequent training is built and as such, if everything has been taught correctly and learnt by the dog, both handler and dog will now be ready for the next stages of training.

Much of the basic training in terms of *'Taking Control'* has involved simple, if not easy, exercises where separate pieces of training are taught and then added to others to form a complete and desirable aspect of work. *'Further Control'* develops work already achieved and shows how to teach a dog further aspects required of a gundog.

For many dogs, and people, the standard of behaviour desirable in a young dog which has achieved the basics, will be sufficient. A dog will have already learnt most aspects of training and a handler will have learnt how to handle their particular dog to the best effect. There is more, however, to be learnt and *'Further Control'* deals with what could be termed the polish but also deals with aspects which inevitably go wrong and areas which are not, perhaps, as bright and shiny as they could be!

You are about to set out, with your dog, on the next part of your journey.

Destinations or goals are important, are exciting, are necessary but frequently become a disappointment when actually reached or achieved. The disappointment is largely because on completion of the journey, reaching the goal or destination there is nothing else to strive for, nowhere to go, nothing to reach for. It is, for many people, the striving, journeying, working aspects of trying to reach a goal that are important and if no longer able to do this, because the goal is reached, people mourn the loss of this activity, consequently the apparent disappointment in the attained goal.

So, please think about the goals; what you want to achieve, what you want to teach your dog, what you want your dog to learn but also enjoy the journey, enjoy each training session you have with your dog and try and enjoy your dog for what he or she is now. Dwell on the qualities of your dog, think of all your dog can do because the lifetime journey of living and working with one particular dog is very short and it is certainly too short to be thinking continually of everything your dog can't do!

A variety of photographs have been used to introduce chapters and for demonstration purposes. I have used photographs of some of the dogs I consider my friends. No significance should be placed on which dog is used for illustration and demonstration purposes.

I hope you enjoy this next part of the journey as much as I have enjoyed writing about it and as much as I continue as an instructor to enjoy the privilege of accompanying other people and lots of dogs on their own personal journeys.

I wish you all well.

Anthea Lawrence

Further Control

(Photograph: Anthea Lawrence)

Parsifal Prelude, a 3yr old Flat Coated retriever and Mistybrook Breeze of Courtridge, a 2yr old Golden retriever.

Best friends Nuala and Gemma

Learning more about *'sit' means sit no matter what......'*

Anthea Lawrence

CHAPTER ONE

Willow
(Photograph: Anthea Lawrence)

The Use and Abuse of the Stop Whistle

First of all, to avoid any confusion, I need to explain that the 'stop' whistle command is the same command as the command to 'sit', which is one short toot on the whistle.

So far your dog will have learnt:

- When he is at heel, the command (of one toot on the whistle) means 'sit'.

- If the dog is already sitting, at a distance, the command means 'watch me, I'm going to tell you what to do'.

If you have been careful both in your teaching and in terms of consistency your dog will also have learnt to relax after a sit command has been given because he knows that neither he nor you will do anything until, and unless, another command is given. Other things may happen around but the dog knows he can simply sit and watch whatever is happening. The dog has therefore learnt that *'sit means sit, no matter what …….'* You too will have learnt that you can watch anything happening around, secure in the knowledge that your dog is relaxed, watching and waiting until you give him a command to do something *different* from what he is doing or the reminder command to *continue* what he is already doing.

Commands are the way in which we communicate with a dog, they are words, whistle and hand signals used as a means of telling a dog what they must do. Commands are also used: as a reminder to a dog to continue doing whatever he is doing; as a reminder to continue doing something because you, the handler, are going to do something else, and/or someone else/another dog is to do something which he (your dog) is to have no part in.

For some reason, many people feel that when they begin to use the whistle to communicate to the dog that he must stop, look at you and wait until told what he should do next, that they have to blow the whistle for as long and as loud as they can. They don't! People have neither to do this, nor *should* do this any more than they should *say* a sit command one minute and **shout** it the next!

The whistle command should be exactly the same every time it is given *except*, that the volume needs to be increased in relation to the distance between the handler and the dog. At heel, the volume needs to be very low whereas further away, the volume needs to increase. In this way the command sounds the same to the dog, who should be in no doubt what it means, as he has been taught what it means.

The command should never be seen as some kind of punishment and yet, by the time this part of training occurs many handlers immediately start to blow the whistle in a different kind of way.

Further Control

It is pure panic on the part of the handler and, instead of the command simply meaning to the dog 'sit', the tone of the whistle can begin to have threatening over-tones and begin to mean *'you had better stop as soon as I blow this whistle or else…'*.

This then conveys to the dog that this whistle command does not mean 'sit' and it must consequently mean something else. The dog does not know what the 'something else' could be and in his dilemma he will anxiously try to do 'something else'. Whatever he does will be wrong because he should sit and his 'something else' will always involve doing something inappropriate, from the handler's point of view.

A vicious circle can then develop and all sorts of things will go wrong; not because the dog is being disobedient, not because the dog is stupid, but simply because a handler has changed into something alien to the dog – one who expects the dog to do something he has not been taught.

You will, by this stage, be well used to using the whistle as a 'sit' command in heel work, and you will have used the whistle also as a 'watch me' command when the dog is sitting at a distance from you and you are going to give another command such as 'go back', 'get on' or a recall.

Those of you who have worked through all the exercises in *'Taking Control'*, will remember that, when practising and developing the recall command, I suggested you should begin to stop your dog with a whistle command *before* he gets all the way back to you on a recall. You will also have begun, when the dog returns to you with a dummy, to get a stop whistle command in before the dog gets all the way back to you on returning.

At those basic stages the use of the stop whistle was to give further experience to a dog in terms of *sit means sit* and also as a way of showing the dog that he must obey the last command given to him even though he has not completed the command given beforehand. This was also preparation however, for further development in the future.

Well, the future has now arrived and has turned into the present!

What we are aiming for, is to be able to send a dog away at speed and then when and if necessary, re-direct a dog, at distance. You cannot re-direct a dog at distance unless the dog stops and looks at you, so that he will know what you want him to do or where you want him to go. It is this aspect of a properly trained gun dog, which will distinguish him from a dog who may well be a very good game finder, but who works to please himself, or will work inefficiently in the wrong place, at the wrong time.

People vary in the way they introduce the stop whistle, some do it early and some late. I prefer to teach almost everything else to a dog first, and introduce the true *stop* whistle command at a fairly late stage apart that is, from the early build up of the whistle commands described earlier.

My reason for this is that I prefer not to have too many battles with my dogs. Insisting a dog stops, sits and watches me from a distance, is not easily accomplished when the dog is charging round a wood at a great speed. Those of you, who are able to run a mile in under 3 minutes, may be able to get out to your dog and use some kind of technique to get the dog's attention but I see no point. This was certainly the way I was taught initially in that the stop whistle was given when the dog was running away from the handler, at speed. Inevitably, many dogs paid no attention to the fact that the whistle had been blown and therefore carried on regardless. The advice given then was for the handler to run out to the dog as quickly as possible, screaming and shouting, bring the dog to a halt by using a technique similar to a rugby tackle, pull the dog's ear, make the dog sit, and then blast the stop-whistle command as loudly as possible into the dog's ear!

Further Control

All of these techniques are beyond me physically and emotionally and totally opposite to the way I now believe is correct. Using these techniques conveys all the wrong messages to the dog in my opinion. Think pack! A dog which is charging around a wood or field, not under the control of the handler (pack leader), is far more likely to go even further afield if the situation is handled in this way. What I saw, years ago, was that although a few dogs understood and learnt, there appeared little improvement with many dogs and there were far more dogs which ran even further away. I saw the results, but at that time did not understand why. Now I understand why!
(See *'Taking Control'*. Chapter Thirteen Going for walks and free play)

Now, I prefer to build up gradually and make life easy for *myself*. I also believe that using a stop whistle in the old way *knowing*, or assuming that the dog will not obey, is part of the old dog breaking techniques and I do not believe in punishment as a way of teaching a dog something. Yes dogs also learn by punishment but I believe that this should only be used *after* I have taught the dog something and at a stage when I know the dog knows the lesson taught. Punishment would then be used as a consequence of the dog disobeying me and not as an initial teaching tool.

I like to believe that this is easier too for the dog, but I acknowledge that dogs learn by whatever methods are favoured by an instructor or handler. I have to live with myself however and believe in being honest with a dog as well as trying everything I can to ensure a dog totally understands the lesson I am trying to teach before ever resorting to punishment of a physical nature, however mild this may be! This takes time and it also depends on reading the dog. Every dog is different and even within the same breed there are huge differences in the rate at which one dog will learn one aspect of training in comparison with another dog. The differences in learning abilities and rates are numerous in dogs and of infinite proportions in people!

Before beginning these exercises it is important to examine the aspects of training, already covered, regarding the foundations of whistle work. You need to make a realistic assessment of yourself and the dog making sure that the dog is responding instantly *come what may*, to each whistle command you give him. If you cannot look at yourself and your dog in this way, get someone else to do the assessment and then do some work on any areas which may need some tidying up before trying to progress.

You should take particular note of how you blow your whistle and get others to monitor whether you ever change the simple one toot command other than a change in volume. The way the whistle is blown should never vary. It is the same as giving a verbal command of 'sit' and as such, should be given in the same tone, every time it is given. It should not change due to circumstances, and it is the change of circumstances which, for some reason, makes handlers change when they should not.

Up to this point you have expected the dog to look at you simply because, apart from at heel, you always blow the whistle and wait for the dog to look before you give a further command. So you have in effect been commanding the dog to look at you and he has learnt that until he does look, nothing is going to happen. After a certain time, you will start to notice the dog looking to you for help on occasions when you haven't commanded him to look say, for example, when he is hunting. He may have searched and not found a dummy and you may suddenly notice he stops and looks at you saying in effect, *'I can't find it, and can you help me?'* This look may be extremely brief and it is important for handlers to watch out for this type of behaviour and try not to miss opportunities presented.

If you watch for any kind of situation when your dog does this, you can quickly get a 'good boy' in and then help him. It is important to praise this action by the dog. You will be rewarding the dog for a different reason than rewards given up to this point, which are for

Further Control

obeying your commands; this reward will be for the dog acting appropriately, thinking for himself and controlling himself in a situation in which he was having some difficulty. This is a very useful indicator that your dog sees you as part of a double act, the pair of you are a team, each valuing the contribution that the other team member can give although you, as leader, will always have the final word. Seeing this *'can you help me?'* question, at this stage of training, will show a handler that the dog is ready for this development of the stop whistle.

To remind you, the command on which you will be working is one toot on the whistle.

Most of the training has already occurred in basic set exercises. It has also happened in other ways, such as the dog learning, by repetition of actions, that when he hears that particular whistle command:

- When he is walking, he must sit instantly.
- When he hears the command when he *is* sitting, he must watch the handler because something else is going to happen *after* he looks at his handler.

The ultimate use of the stop whistle, apart from those areas already mentioned, is to be able to stop your dog, at a distance, when the dog is actively doing something. Many people refer to this as the 'brakes', which means the whistle is the handler's way of stopping the dog.

Many novice handlers have problems with this use of the whistle. I believe this is because they immediately attach some kind of negative meaning to the purpose of the command. By this, I mean that they see the command, not as a positive means of calling a halt to the first thing a dog has done correctly and to be able then to give the dog something else to do, but a command to mean *'I am going to stop this dog, and I am determined that he will stop, come what may!'* They are thinking, before they even start, that it is a command to be used because the dog is doing something wrong, or something the handler does not want the dog to do.

A handler therefore begins, feeling that the command is to be used as a form of punishment. Everything about their body language and the way that the whistle is blown portrays this feeling too and it consequently conveys this message to the dog that in turn, finds it difficult to comprehend the sudden change in attitude.

There may well be times in the future that a whistle command has to be given to a dog because the dog is doing something you do not want him to do. The command itself must remain what it is and that is simply a command to *'stop, look at me because I am going to tell you what to do or help you'*.

This command, the same as all other commands, should never be used as a punishment and it is important for handlers to keep this in mind before attempting to try the command out when the dog is at a distance and on the move.

It is far better at a later stage to stop a dog *before* he does something wrong and dogs who have learnt that the stop whistle is not a punishment and simply a command to sit, will respond much more quickly because they will have learnt that they are immediately praised for so doing. Handlers will therefore be in a much better position to actually prevent a dog doing something that is not required, or prevent a dog running into danger because the dog will have learnt to stop immediately in order to get his praise.

In this way you can send your dog away from you say on a 'go back' command, realise that the dog has perhaps gone too far, or may be approaching some danger, blow the stop whistle, praise the dog for his obedience, and then command him to go in some other direction or recall him.

Further Control

The command should always be seen as a positive measure. This is all to do with timing as well as anticipation by the handler, who should not wait until a dog is doing something wrong whenever possible. If a handler is alert, reading their dog correctly and able to see the likelihood that the dog may be about to do something wrong; then the handler can act appropriately by stopping the dog preferably *before* he does something wrong or the instant he *starts* doing something wrong.

If the stop whistle is seen by the handler as just a command, it is more likely that the dog will obey it. If the dog does not obey it however, once he knows what it means, then the handler has the right to punish the dog in some way.

Using the command itself as a punishment is unjust and extremely confusing to a dog if he has been taught, up to this point, that he must obey every command and will be praised if he does and punished if he doesn't. Those are the ground rules you have been teaching *for life!*

You should never try to use the stop whistle, just to see if it works, prior to doing the following build-up exercises. If you try, the likelihood is that it will not work.

All you will do is teach the dog that he can ignore your whistle when he is at a distance from you and, perhaps more importantly, you will show your dog, very clearly, that you have no control over him when he is on the move and at a distance from you. This control aspect, or lack of it, is not something you need or want the dog to realise, and learn!

Throughout training a handler needs to convey to a dog that wherever the dog is in relation to the handler, it is the handler who controls everything *'no matter what…..'*

The *'no matter what'* will continue to mean the same as it has meant from the start:

- 🐾 No matter what I am doing.
- 🐾 No matter what you are doing.
- 🐾 No matter what other people are doing.
- 🐾 No matter what other dogs are doing.
- 🐾 No matter what circumstances we are in.
- 🐾 No matter what livestock there may be around.
- 🐾 No matter how exciting life becomes.
- 🐾 No matter what you would prefer to do instead.

In fact *'no matter what……………………………………'*

Willow
(Photograph: Anthea Lawrence)

Further Control

CHAPTER TWO

Dolly
(Photograph: Mary Ward)

The Stop Whistle – Training and Exercises

Much of the teaching concerning the stop whistle has already been accomplished in basic training. Before going onto this particular aspect however, handlers should ensure that the dog's learning is in fact up to the level the handler feels he has taught. The two things are not necessarily the same! These are the circumstances which have already been taught on the whistle:

- When walking to heel on and off the lead. The handler halts and the dog will sit immediately on one whistle toot.

- When walking to heel off the lead, the handler gives one whistle toot and keeps walking. The dog sits immediately and makes no attempt to keep walking with the handler or move. (Described as a 'quick sit' in *Taking Control*')

- When sitting at a distance from the handler the dog will remain in a sit *no matter what,* and on one whistle toot will look at the handler but not move until given a command to do something other than sit.

If none, or only some, of the above is true it will be necessary to do some further work on any aspect where there is a problem, before continuing. It is important not to proceed with any aspects of training until a dog shows he understands what he has been taught up to that point and a handler is doing everything appropriately and consistently. Problems in training do not go away, they only get worse!

Although the aim is to use the stop whistle when the dog is going away from the handler I find it best to start teaching this use of the command when the dog is coming towards me. In this way I have a little more control if things go wrong! Also, by this stage of training, you should have: a dog which wants to come back to you quickly and a dog which has no fear of doing this, because of the praise he has had all his life.

You need simply to teach the dog that the command is the same when he is moving, on his own at a distance from you; if, to begin with, he is moving away from the handler, the handler may have little chance of enforcing the command if the dog ignores it. So, show him on a recall first.

Those of you who have worked through the exercises in *'Taking Control'* will remember that, in the distant past when you first tried a whistle recall command, I mentioned then, that I have 2 recall commands. Now is the time to start the 'come towards me' command, if you intend to use 2 types of recall. If you have not yet used this command, then you can start using now if you wish. The command brings the dog forward slowly on a *'come towards me, as I am going to give you another command and/or help you'* basis, instead of a *'come back to me as quickly as you*

Further Control 17

can' for the quick recall. You cannot use this however if you use a similar command as a hunting/'hie lost' command.

As usual, when teaching something new, it is better to go to an unexciting training area.

Sit your dog up and move 10/15 paces away and turn to face the dog ready to do a basic recall.

Think before you do anything. You are going to slow recall the dog and blow your stop whistle to make the dog sit *before* he gets all the way back to you. Don't assume that your dog will do this the first time. If you blow your stop whistle and the dog continues to come to you, you and the dog will have gained nothing. Assume that the dog will not stop!

When you turn to face the dog, do everything practised so far, i.e. hand signal, whistle (look at me), then blow the slow recall whistle. When the dog starts moving, say *'good boy'* (for obeying the recall) and immediately blow the stop whistle (gently) as well as giving the hand signal to sit.

At the same time as you blow the stop whistle, you must start moving forward so that you are moving towards the incoming dog. Keep your hand and arm up as you go but do not blow the whistle again. This command, like all other commands must be obeyed on the first and only command given. By keeping your hand and arm up, you will hopefully indicate to the dog that you want him to sit *out there*, where he is when he hears the whistle.

Some dogs sit almost instantly but others take longer, and you may have to go right up to the dog before he obeys. Once the dog sits, even if you are virtually on top of him you must give a lot of verbal praise. Many handlers at this point do not praise sufficiently, their reason being that *'well, the dog didn't stop when I told him to'*. This shows a handler's lack of understanding about their own job as trainer to the dog. The dog cannot understand that a whistle sound means 'sit' in these circumstances because these circumstances have not been learnt in conjunction with the command. This is all part of doing the same things in many different circumstances so that the command never changes but the circumstances go on changing. The dog therefore needs to learn all about commands being applied in different circumstances and to do this he needs praise to say *yes, you're doing the right thing.*

The other problem when teaching this exercise and this is a problem for the dog so something handlers should be wary of, and that is of handlers moving forward towards the incoming dog but glaring at the dog in a menacing manner. It is much better for handlers to adopt a neutral expression but even more important, the handler should look at the place the dog should stop, which is somewhere on the ground, and never look directly at the dog. In this way you are pointing with your eyes concerning something you want to happen.

It is important to remember you are teaching the dog something new, even though you may not feel it *is* new. To the dog it is new and as such, as soon as the dog obeys your command, he must be praised otherwise he will never learn what you want.

Keep the dog sitting, back away to your starting point and then praise the dog again. At this stage go back to the dog, praise again and walk him to heel back to his original position. Try the exercise another couple of times and on each occasion, follow the same procedure of going forward to meet the dog. You must only blow the whistle once on each occasion.

What you will find sometimes, is that your dog may be reluctant or hesitant to obey the recall whistle after the first or second try, so it is vital that you get plenty of praise in when he obeys the recall and before you blow the stop whistle. If I witness this reluctance or hesitation I

Further Control

always view it as a good sign! It means that the dog is thinking that he will be stopped which means he is already using the thought process which I am trying to teach.

So if this happens, don't worry about it. Once the dog has processed the whole aspect, he will get the new information sorted out in his mind and the recall will fall back into place as it was before. This is, of course, if you made sure that the recall command was being obeyed instantly, prior to starting this new aspect!

You may have to have several sessions on this exercise (maximum of 3 attempts each session) before your dog understands fully. Your aim will be to build up distance so that from the recall position you can stand still, recall the dog and get him to sit at distance, immediately you blow the stop whistle. Vary the distances and vary at which point you blow the whistle. By using praise, and being ready to go forward each time, the dog will soon understand, and it is an exercise whereby you can increase his awareness of obeying the last command you have given, even though he has not completed the first command you gave. This will only happen if you continue to praise all the correct actions by the dog.

Do not be tempted to rush ahead with the use of the stop whistle. When having the first few sessions of this, reinforce the use of the whistle on all the other exercises too and build up the dog's confidence and understanding gradually. Having got this far there is no point in letting the dog think that the stop whistle, in these circumstances, is some kind of punishment – it is not, and it is up to you as leader, and hopefully as the more intelligent of the partnership, to show the dog that it is simply a command, which he already knows, but it is being used in other circumstances. As with all commands, it must be obeyed.

Once the dog will stop on recall immediately you blow the whistle and will stop wherever commanded, vary things a little so that something happens immediately the dog stops. You can do this by throwing a dummy to the side, or firing a shot.

In this way the dog begins to associate stopping with the fact that sometimes there is another purpose for stopping as well as the need to obey the command. It is also a way of maintaining the interest of the dog because training is better accomplished by keeping the interest factors, keeping the excitement, as well as furthering the circumstances in which you have control.

You can also vary what happens next after the dog sits at a distance. Sometimes you should recall the dog again, this time using your rapid toots recall; sometimes go back to the dog and walk him to heel in another direction; send him for a thrown dummy on occasions, but never for every dummy thrown.

I should add here, that if you have thrown a dummy or fired a shot, and you then intend to recall the dog: you must be alert to the fact that your dog may want to go and investigate. The dog must obey the recall whistle no matter what has happened and you should bear this in mind.

Once the dog has gone to investigate it is too late in many ways, so be attentive and make sure that any deviation by the dog is addressed by you early!

Further developments.

When your dog is obeying a stop whistle immediately, and happily, on a recall, you will know that it is time to develop this further. The real test is whether the dog has understood that the whistle means 'sit' no matter what he is doing or where he is and no matter what you may be doing or where you are in relation to him.

Further Control

Your next step will be to send the dog away from you and then blow the stop whistle but don't just rush out and try it! As with other aspects of training, this needs to be built up slowly.

The way I was taught to do this originally was to use a marked retrieve: a mark was thrown, the dog sent in the normal way for a marked retrieve but the stop whistle was blown by the handler, before the dog got to the dummy. I do not recommend that anyone tries this method but if you do try it you should make sure you have someone with you who can throw the dummy but more importantly, can pick up the dummy before the dog gets it, if the dog does not stop on the whistle. The dog should not get the reward of the dummy if he has disobeyed the stop whistle! Preferably do not do it as above!

I found that there were problems with this method in that many dogs would ignore the stop whistle and even if a dummy was picked up before the dog got to it, the dog would go on hunting where he thought it was. Handlers would then be told to get out to the dog, bring it to a halt, by whatever means were available, and then drag the dog back to the place the dog should have stopped and finally, blast the whistle in the dog's ear.

I hated doing this then, and I hate it even more now when I witness other people doing it and yes, - it is still happening in gundog training sessions all over the country! Not in mine, I hasten to add!

I now prefer to take a different approach because using physical abuse is not necessary. It is unjust to the dog, causes stress in both dog and human and this type of stress is not conducive to learning in either human or dog. There are also other reasons why this method is, in my view, unsatisfactory:

> 🐾 If you have already taught the dog that for a mark you want the dog to go straight out on a name command only and

retrieve the mark quickly, I see no point in changing this philosophy at any stage.

If you start interfering with this, in terms of teaching the dog that *sometimes* you will send the dog for the mark but will stop him before he gets it, some dogs lose the confidence to go immediately to a mark and will go some distance and then stop and look at their handler for confirmation or an *'are you going to stop me?'* question.

This hesitation can mean the dog forgets where the mark landed but it also means a handler must then give another command after the dog has stopped. This is not a situation which we want, and should not be a situation we create.

I can think of no circumstances where this situation would be likely to occur in the shooting field. I know some people who say *'oh well, if you've sent your dog for a shot, dead bird he has seen land, but another wounded bird comes down before your dog has retrieved the dead bird, then you would want to stop your dog and re-direct him to the wounded one'*. Well, I'm afraid I would not.

To me it is pointless. If I have made the decision to send my dog for a bird then that is what I want the dog to do. In most circumstances it is likely that I would only send the dog during the drive, for a bird which I thought may be wounded. If my dog was half-way to retrieve that bird I would never try to pull him off that one to go for another bird, which may be wounded. That could result in neither bird being retrieved.

I firmly believe that *a bird in the hand* or in this case, a bird in the dog's mouth and then in my hand, is preferable to two birds possibly being lost.

I do not believe in being dishonest with a dog. Throughout training a handler needs to be consistent and right from the very start of training, get the dog to understand that one command will always mean a certain action for ever. In this way the dog learns to trust his handler. As

Further Control

training progresses, commands will be expanded to encompass more of the same or different circumstances where the command applies but the basic action taught will remain the same.

If the name command means *'go quickly to retrieve the dummy you have seen thrown or the bird you have seen shot'*, I believe it is dishonest to send a dog for a mark on the name command when I know, right from the start, that I am going to stop the dog before he retrieves that mark.

Changing this to a 'go back' command would be more honest, but that too will create doubt in the dog's mind. If a thrown dummy is used it would mean the handler is changing the definition on the action required from the dog for what he perceives as a marked dummy, even if the word 'mark' is not used.

You should have, at this stage a dog which will go immediately, on its name, to retrieve a mark where you do nothing: no stepping forward, no flinging your arms in the air, no looking at the dog, no conversation, no nothing *except;* that you and the dog keep your eyes forward watching the mark from start to the finish.

You then say one word (the dog's name); your dog goes with speed straight to the fall, retrieves the item, comes back to you at speed, presents the item to you and then waits for the next command.

Wow, that's impressive! Well I think it is impressive!

It took a long time, with careful building up of every stage from when the dog was about 4 months old. You and the dog have got marks sorted! It gets no better than this! Many people would give anything, part with a lot of money to achieve this. I wish someone would tell me why, now, anyone would want to destroy this creation which has been carefully, patiently and caringly built?

To teach another circumstance to the dog, where the stop whistle applies, is necessary. Going away from you to retrieve a marked bird or dummy is *not* another circumstance where the stop whistle should apply.

The only time it may apply is if you have sent your dog as normal, but your dog does not find the bird! Then you may need to stop the dog and either re-direct, in some circumstances, or recall. You would not be using the whistle whilst the dog was on his way out however! Re-directing should not happen on a regular basis and in training if the dog does not go straight to a marked retrieve then he should be recalled and the mark thrown again. Dogs should not be handled on a marked retrieve otherwise they give up watching and marking correctly.

It makes no sense to teach a dog about the stop whistle by using a marked retrieve and I now do it as follows: take the dog to a track (as set up for blinds, and if possible use the same track as you have used for this purpose in the past) but do not put a dummy on the track.

Line the dog up for a 'go back' and send the dog in the usual way, as if there was a dummy out. When the dog has gone a short distance, blow the stop whistle (gently) and be ready to go forward, behind the dog, in case he doesn't stop, and he may not because this is a new circumstance:

> If the dog stops instantly, praise immediately and then, with the dog still sitting at distance from you, repeat the sit command as a reminder, with praise, say *'mark'* and throw a dummy over your head, behind you.

Repeat the stop whistle and hand signal to the dog and watch the dog all the time. Don't watch the dummy. Praise the dog and then go to him and praise again. You can then go round the dog into the heel position, line the dog up and send him on a 'go back' to retrieve the dummy you have just thrown. Do not do any more on that session but

Further Control

do some other training and wait to develop this further on a subsequent session.

> 🐾 If the dog does not stop immediately.

You need to be already moving towards the dog as you blow the whistle and having blown the whistle once, be ready immediately to go to the dog and growl at him (for disobeying you).

When you get to the dog, put the dog on a lead and take him back to the point at which he *should have stopped*. There is no need to do this in a rough or punishing way as the growl should have been sufficient for the dog to understand that he has done something wrong.

Neither though, should you speak to the dog; just take him back on the lead to where he should have been if he had obeyed you. It is important to take the dog back and put him on the exact spot he had reached, when you blew the whistle.

You do not want to teach him that when you blow the whistle he can go another 6 yards, or more, before he must stop. This is an occasion when you show him that he should not go even 6 inches more!

Take the lead off, blow your stop whistle (gently) as a reminder and also give a verbal *'sit'* command and praise for obeying. Leave the dog on that spot and then return to your original position.

At this point you will probably be cross. So, try not to be, calm down, take a deep breath and say *'mark'* whilst throwing a dummy behind you.

Watch the dog, not the dummy, and reinforce the whistle command with a hand signal and then praise the dog. Go back to the dog, praise him and you go and pick up the dummy, leaving your dog sitting. Return to the dog and praise, take a deep breath and start again.

This will hopefully show your dog several things (a) what you want him to do when you blow the whistle (b) that when he stops at a distance something else may happen and (c) that you will teach him what is required in the same way as you have done all his life, with ordinary commands, with praise for when he is correct and a growl as punishment when he is wrong.

In this way he will learn what you want and it is important for handlers to remember they are teaching, and teaching takes as long as it takes for the dog to learn. You can't speed up the learning process by excessive punishment or by getting cross – both those things lengthen the learning process.

- Walk the dog to heel, back to the original starting point, and try the exercise, in exactly the same way as before.

Most dogs will stop on command on this second attempt or some may hesitate, go a bit further and then sit. Others may hesitate but not sit but whatever the dog does will hopefully be a slight improvement on the previous attempt. Remember you are trying to teach the dog what you require and with some dogs this will take time and a lot of patience.

If necessary, try the exercise 3 times. The dog will learn: if you are patient and help the dog with the correct use of lots of praise for any attempt to obey and a quick growl if the dog disobeys. After 3 attempts, even if the dog has not managed to complete the exercise, do no more for that session but do some more training on things your dog knows, and can do.

Finish on something which the dog understands and then let him have a think about the new bit.

On subsequent sessions, once the dog is stopping immediately, follow the exercise as in above for *'If the dog stops instantly'*.

Further Control

Don't do too much stopping on the whistle – it can make dogs what we call 'sticky', which means they are reluctant to follow commands for as long as you want because they are expecting to be stopped. As with all training exercises it is important to teach for as long as the dog needs to learn without getting cross, without punishing the dog in any way other than growling instantly the dog goes wrong but above all praising every aspect which is correct.

Once the dog will stop using this exercise, you can vary things a little by incorporating things such as a shot or throwing a mark in another direction such as to the side or in front of the dog. Sometimes you can send the dog for a dummy, or pick it up yourself and sometimes recall the dog so that he learns he cannot always retrieve when he has seen a dummy thrown.

If training with others you can try stopping one dog at a distance, throwing the dummy and sending another dog to retrieve it. Then the order can be reverse so that you stop the other dog at a distance, throw the dummy and then send the first dog to retrieve.

Always try to finish a training session with something easy, which the dog knows, so you can both be happy to finish on success. Dogs love continuing to do the easy, puppy-training exercises. Even much older ones enjoy a 'go back' across a field or through a wood and they don't seem to get bored with it. So, find the things which your dog enjoys and is good at and let him finish with something which makes him happy and on which you know you will not have to do any correction or teaching.

Something worthwhile which makes the dog happy, will also make you happy you'll find and a happy trainer and a happy and contented dog works best for teaching and learning. You can both go home dwelling on how wonderful the training session was, even if the new bit was a disaster! Next time, you will find the new bit won't be such a disaster because it won't be the new bit next time and dogs appear to learn a lot from thinking between sessions!

Handlers too, learn from thinking after training sessions and it is useful for you to do this, particularly if something has gone wrong or not been as simple as you thought it would be. Think how you can make it easier for the dog to learn what you are trying to teach, make any adjustments in your own skills or technique and above all do not get cross when trying to teach. Sometimes you may have to act as though you were cross, but this should never be a reality.

You will find, once the stop whistle has been practiced with success on these set exercises that you can incorporate it into your training sessions and it will simply become a part of every day life.

Once a dog is perfectly steady and ready for more complex retrieving situations, gradually build up the use of the whistle but use it *only* if you need to! Also, use it only when you are in a position to do something about the situation, should your dog disobey.

For dogs which are not 100% reliable on the stop whistle, there is no point in sending the dog across a river, for example, and then blowing the stop whistle. If the dog does not obey, you cannot do a great deal to explain!

So use it with care.

One final point; once a dog knows what a stop whistle means, and he is reliable in terms of responding to it, there may not be the need for you to insist on the dog sitting when he hears it.

Some dogs continue to sit on the stop whistle all their lives and others begin simply to turn on the spot and wait for their next command.

Further Control

If speed is essential, and this may be because of a wounded bird, then I feel it is pointless in wasting precious seconds waiting for a dog to sit before giving the next command.

At this stage of training the one toot whistle should simply start to mean, *'stop there, look at me and wait for me to tell you what to do next'*. The 'sit' part of this was necessary as an initial teaching tool but not necessarily part of the finished product.

That does not mean, of course, that a dog should be allowed to disobey a subsequent command to sit after the stop whistle or at any other time, and this should be put in on occasions when training, to ensure the dog does not forget. As long as the dog has understood the definition of stopping, that is the most important aspect and the fact of whether the dog sits at that point, is purely a matter of personal choice.

If there is any inclination by the dog to anticipate your next command or only to stop *eventually*, or do anything other than stop immediately then it would be necessary, I feel, to return to insisting the dog sits on the stop whistle. If he is sitting, he cannot go anywhere!

There are times when I have seen and heard handlers, when handling their dogs at great distances, wasting a lot of time and effort in trying to shout a *'sit'* command to the dog after the dog has stopped. The dog is quite clearly not going anywhere, is looking for the next command, possibly cannot hear the handler's voice and just wants to be told what to do.

If the dog, as above, is doing all the right things and doing everything a handler could desire, then I believe there is no point in trying to give a sit command or expecting the dog to sit. This is not an excuse for sloppy handling however! Handlers should never give a different, subsequent command to a dog if the dog has ignored a stop whistle.

The handler must insist on the stop and/or sit first before giving the subsequent, different command of 'go back', 'get on' or whatever.

Dolly
(Photograph: Mary Ward)

Further Control

The stop whistle

Lily
(Photograph: David Tomlinson)

When the dog has been stopped at a distance, she should turn quickly on the spot and look at the handler: *'Yes? What do you want me to do? Where do you want me to go?'*

Teaching a dog to sit when the stop whistle is given is necessary at the beginning of training but later, when out working, it is often the case that one wants the dog to go quickly in another direction – in this case for a wounded duck in the ditch! Stopping the dog and re-directing her to the correct area is more important than the dog sitting. It is the stopping which is important by this stage of training, so that the handler can give the next command and send the dog to the correct area before the wounded duck is lost. It is not vital that the dog sits at a distance: however, if there is any unsteadiness shown, or anticipation of what your next command may be, it would be necessary to reinforce the sit to deal with these difficulties.

CHAPTER THREE

Nuala
(Photograph: Anthea Lawrence)

Hunting and Scent

Hunting is something which gundogs usually enjoy because it means that not only can they scurry around 'looking' for something but, joy of joys, get to give full reign to the one sense which they enjoy the most - scent. Scent is like a drug to a gundog but scent also acts as his 'eyes' in that catching the scent of something enables the dog to locate it in a far more efficient way than using sight.

There may appear occasions when we humans use words in gundog circles which appear to contradict the normally accepted meaning of words connected with the senses. A lot of it has become jargon which is fine if you know, but appears like a secret language to outsiders and those new to the sport and wishing to become insiders. All activities have their own secret language but there is nothing sinister about it, it is simply a way of conveying a precise meaning to something.

Further Control

If you have spent time watching dogs and you are beginning to understand dog language, you will have noticed that dogs look with their nose, and they point with their eyes. If you doubt this in any way just watch your dog trying to find something and you can hear him smelling, taking huge breaths to take in as much scent as he can and to taste it.

If your dog wants something, which either you or another dog has, he will look at the object intensely. In the same way as a young child will point with his finger at a biscuit and say *'me want'*, a dog stares at something and is trying to say *'me want'*. Dogs also use their eyes to indicate *'I am not going to touch whatever you've got, under any circumstances'*, by looking away with their eyes but also by deliberately turning their heads away from the object in question. Watch dogs together when one has a bone or toy, or watch young dogs do this when they are learning what the 'leave it' command means. As soon as they understand, they move their heads to avert their eyes, and that tells a handler that their dog has fully understood the meaning of the command.

The other slightly puzzling word we use is that of a dog 'touching' scent. How on earth do you touch scent? You don't, but dogs do!

All it means is that if you watch very closely, you can see the precise moment when a dog locates the first scent of something for which it is hunting. There may be a slight turn of the head, there may be a slight falter in movement and with some dogs the tail will move in a different way or they will turn their head and put their nose more fully in the direction from which the scent is coming.

One of my dogs turns her tail over in complete circles when she finds something after a hunt; something she never does in other circumstances. It is this split second change in the dog's body language or behaviour, which handlers should learn to recognise and this is termed as 'touching scent'. Blink and you may miss it, but it is significant!

Sight is more efficient in the dog if the object being looked for moves. If you are in any doubt about this you only have to observe a dog hunting for a dummy or bird when you can see the item quite clearly but the dog appears not to notice. A dog can even step on a dummy or bird and not know it is there.

The reason for this apparent 'over-looking' the item is simply due to the fact that the dog did not pick up any scent from the item either as he was approaching it or as he was passing by. As a consequence, to the dog, the item is not there.

If no scent is picked up by the dog he will continue hunting until he locates scent or he will give up, or try somewhere else. If, however, the object for which he is hunting suddenly gets up and moves or runs or blinks an eye, then the slightest movement will be sufficient for the dog to be alerted and he will be drawn to where he saw movement before reverting to following the trail of scent. This aspect was a crucial feature for dog packs in the past because following trails of scent was of little value if it did not lead to supper for the day. Supper was always alive and alive meant moving!

Humans have great difficulty in understanding totally, the scenting powers of the dog. More and more information is being gained about the capabilities of dogs; one can only marvel at those dogs which are able to predict epileptic fits, detect cancer cells, discover hoards of illegal drugs or find mines, bombs and explosives. We can marvel but find no real understanding of how it all works and some of it defies belief in that we observe it but, because we have no way of relating this to our own level of ability concerning the senses, we find difficulty in truly believing what we see.

With gundogs we know that on some days, dogs appear to have problems using their sense of scent. Gundog people talk of *'bad scenting days'* meaning that dogs need to *'trip over the dummy'* before they find it.

Further Control

We know that wind has a lot to do with scent, we know also that some ground conditions can mask scent and sometimes, some areas of ground, for some reason, can always be bad for scenting – people call this 'dead ground'. We do not know why however, although many people will have numerous theories.

You have already taught your dog that when he hears the words 'Hie Lost', he finds a dummy or something, which he is to pick up and bring to you. If you have been developing your dog's experience on a marked retrieve, he will have been sent to retrieve dummies which, although he saw the dummy thrown he will not have been able to see on the ground before leaving your side. This is because it has landed just out of sight behind a tree or perhaps into rough grass. Even when he gets to the area where he thinks the dummy will have landed, he may not be able to see it, but he will have found it by using his nose and searching, hunting, when you have said 'Hie Lost'.

These types of retrieve will have taught the dog how clever you are because you knew where the dummy was, and he did not, until you helped him, thus building up trust in you the leader. These retrieves also show the dog that when you say 'Hie Lost' it is worthwhile for him to keep on hunting, because you have always been correct before and he has found something

It is very important, I believe, to maintain this trust and hopefully you will always have disciplined yourself regarding use of commands and setting up training exercises correctly so that things have never gone wrong for the dog. If things have gone wrong you have put it right with an appropriate follow up exercise at the time.

I am never dishonest with dogs and I do not believe in deliberately setting a dog up to fail. I set things up so that the dog succeeds at however minimum a level, and build each step into his training up to that point. If, however hard you try to make this work, it still goes wrong, it is vital to go back and build up again from a suitable point. It is also worth taking the time to think about what you are trying to teach the dog and see whether there may be some smaller steps on the way to the desired aspect you are trying to teach, whereby you can build up more gradually. In this way the dog still trusts; you help him every step of the way and together you succeed.

Hunting training has therefore begun but needs developing and you need to stretch the dog's understanding of the hunting command so he will persevere for longer. It is also important for you to read your dog.

By this I mean you should be building up an understanding of the character, temperament, skills, sensitivity and aspects of your dog which make him the dog he is and which define him as an individual who is unique. He may well have certain aspects which define him as a particular breed of gundog, and it is important for everyone to understand these breed characteristics but within each breed there are thousands of aspects which, when put together in differing combinations, will create a different character dog each time one is born.

No two dogs are the same and handlers who can understand the differences between their dog and others; who understand how their dog should be trained in comparison with others; who understand when to push their dog a little on a training issue and when to back off; are learning to read their dog, and as a consequence will be able to tailor training issues to suit their particular dog.

The inability to read dogs is one of the reasons why many of us have failed in training numerous dogs in the past and most people *have* failed with previous dogs. Very seldom is this because of some innate problem in the dog. Perhaps failing, or not progressing far enough, is a necessary step in our own chain of learning but one constantly hears people in training classes talking about dogs they have owned previously and saying *'if only I had known this training aspect or concept before'*. They then talk about wonderful dogs owned, who for one reason or

Further Control

another have not quite made the grade; been wonderful game finders but would not come back; been extremely clever but would not walk to heel; been extrovert characters who were full of love and fun but chased everything in sight.

For all of us who have had dogs in the past there is a feeling, when we finally have a dog where we have taken control, shown leadership and learned to read the dog, that we should have done it differently before.

There is also a feeling of guilt that we failed a previous dog. Yes, we did in some ways but not due to any deliberate act in most cases, but due to naivety and inexperience. This only becomes apparent when we finally start to get it right with the latest dog which joins the pack. We then begin to value the much greater relationship and bond we have with dogs when we become the true leader, take control and actually keep that control under all circumstances.

For those of you who have worked through everything in *'Taking Control'*: trained your dog since approximately 10 weeks of age, never moving onto the next stage of training until the previous stage was taught to, and learned by, the dog; you should now have a dog receptive to you, looking to you to give commands and a dog who is obeying each and every command you give, instantly, willingly and happily.

It is at this stage that your dog needs to be given a little more freedom to work at a distance from you, perhaps out of sight, and to work for longer on his own without input from you. In other words you start to utilize the skills the dog has brought to the partnership.

If you have a dog which is sensitive and anxious to do everything correctly, he needs to be given opportunities to experience hunting on his own to teach him that no harm will come to him when he ventures further away from you. This type of dog needs to learn about what his nose is telling him and to differentiate between scents. He also needs to learn about strength and weakness of scent and which line to follow to ensure that scent is gaining in strength if he goes in one direction or that scent is weakening in strength if he goes in the opposite direction.

If however, you have a dog who takes every opportunity to hunt for a long time and the further away the better, things need to be refined so that he begins to learn that hunting is fine, but you are still in charge of it all and he may only do it when you say so, where you say so and only for as long as you say so; then he must stop and come back to you immediately he hears the recall command.

Many dogs in this category are not looking or hunting *for* something, but simply enjoying the experience of smelling anything and everything which is there or has been there and left scent. These are the drug addicts of the gundog world and they are not necessarily the best gundogs in the world! These are often too, the dogs which have perhaps been allowed too much freedom in the past to hunt on their own, with no input from a handler and at a time when they were not under the control of their handler.

Handlers must define for themselves a specific area in their mind in which they will use 'Hie Lost', if you are going to use a verbal hunting command, or to give the slow toot whistle command for hunting. I define a length of about 6 feet from where I believe a dummy or bird to be. This means a dog can go in a six foot circle North, East, South or West of the dummy whilst I say 'Hie Lost' and out of that area I would be giving another command.

This means in practice that if, when I have given the 'Hie Lost' command, the dog hunts beyond my 6 feet range, then the dog would be stopped, redirected – left, right, back or slow recall. Then when he was back in the correct area, I would give the 'Hie Lost' command again.

This in reality is a huge area which, if my dim memories of some of the things I retained from maths lessons are to be relied upon, is the

Further Control

area of a circle with a radius of 3 feet, which equals about 28 square feet. I have great difficulty in knowing lengths and distances just by looking and if it is of any help to anyone else with similar problems, I imagine a man lying on the ground, to try and define 6 feet in length in any direction.

This may seem a little complicated to a handler to begin with but you will soon develop your own skills in this as you and the dog learn together. If you have difficulty in defining an area, measure it out, go to the area and pace it out, do anything which will enable you to see distances, lengths and areas. Tie something to two trees which you know are, for example, 25 feet apart and then move 100 yards away and look from there to see what the area looks like from a distance.

The other training aspect which handlers must learn about is wind. Scent for a dog is almost always determined by wind direction and the scent being carried on the wind away from an item required by a handler. I say *almost always* because in some circumstances dogs seem to be able to locate some items with little help from the wind, but due to the sheer volume of the scent generated by the item.

These items are generally the things which we humans would prefer to ignore but to a dog they are irresistible and they will enjoy things such as fox droppings, dead and rotting carcasses, to the full. Most people will have *enjoyed* too, sharing space with a dog dripping in black and slimy green fox droppings and *enjoyed* the experience of trying to get rid of the offending perfume from every crevice of the dog which he has managed to rub in it!

Many novice handlers have difficulty in understanding how crucial wind direction is, and are totally amazed that their dog can almost tread on an item, and not know it is there, until one points out that due to the wind direction, the scent from the item was being carried away on the opposite side from the side the dog was, in relation to the item.

This is much more difficult to describe in writing or verbally, than it is to show by practical means.

Imagine for a moment that you place a dummy on the ground on a breezy day. You then set fire to the dummy and step away a few yards. Watch the smoke and you will see the wind taking the smoke away from the dummy. Scent to the dog is exactly like smoke from a fire.

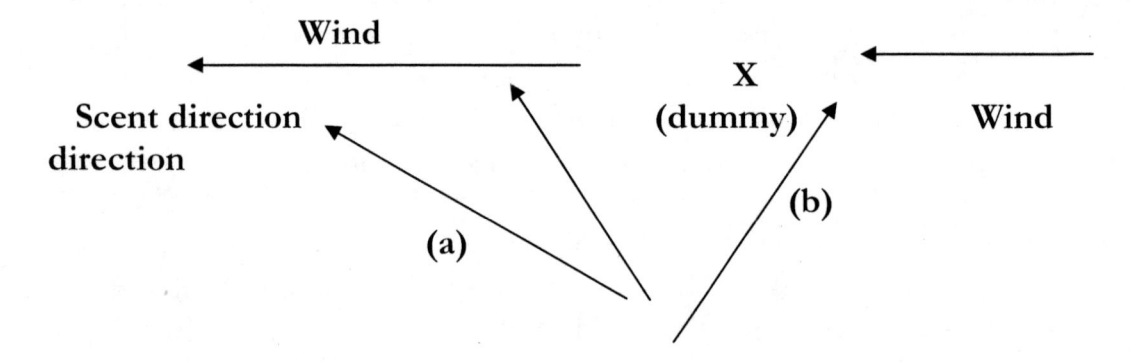

```
                    Wind
        ←─────────────────────              ←──────
                                    X
   Scent direction              (dummy)              Wind
        direction
                                      (b)
              (a)
```

A dog sent on any line to the left of the dummy (a) will pick up the scent of the dummy whether it is a few inches away or if it is on a diagonal line towards the scent line, from many yards away. With experience, he will begin to understand whether the scent is getting weaker when he goes further to his left, because it is further from the dummy, or getting stronger if he goes to his right because he is getting closer to the dummy. A dog sent on line (b) may pass very close to the dummy, but will not pick up the scent. He is more likely therefore to continue running a long way out of the area in which he should be.

I am not suggesting that you go out and set fire to training dummies but a useful and relatively cheap way of demonstrating this is by using a tub of bubble liquid, loved by many children and easily available. Place a dummy on the ground and then blow some bubbles close to the dummy and watch where the wind takes the bubbles. Get someone else to do this whilst you stand further back and watch. Sometimes the wind

Further Control

will be different where you are standing, from how it is near the dummy or bird.

Gaining experience in these matters is crucial for handlers who need to begin thinking of wind much more in these stages of training than they did when teaching basic exercises to dogs. It should begin to be one of the first things thought about from now on when setting up more advanced exercises and particularly when entering competitions of any kind. The more handlers can learn about watching the way grass and leaves are blowing in the distance and gauging the wind on their face or neck, the more successful they will be in sending their dog on the correct line at the start, knowing when to give a hunting command and knowing when to stop a dog and re-direct or when to leave it alone.

Often handlers do not understand the correct time to do something regarding their dog. Either, handlers do too much and won't leave their dog alone to work or they leave things too late, don't do anything and then have to spend a long time with much whistling and re-directing to get their dog to where the dog should be.

Many handlers, due often to thinking too much about competitions, feel they are going to be penalised by judges for blowing their stop whistle and handling. Yes, they are correct in some ways but, and it is a BIG but, they are going to be penalised a great deal more for not blowing their stop whistle and re-directing, when the situation warrants it.

For example, if we take the situation as in the diagram above: If you know approximately where the dummy is (X) and need to send the dog to retrieve it, your first consideration must be the wind direction. The dummy may be hidden from your view but you should send the dog to the left of the dummy because there is much more margin for error on that side than the other.

If you send your dog on a direct line to the dummy and he strays an inch away from it on the right he probably won't find it. If he strays away up to 20 yards, on some days, but on the left, he will catch scent somewhere at the point where he crosses the line of the wind. At that point the dog will turn into the line of scent and find the dummy.

So having sent your dog; if you realise your dog is anywhere on a line to the left, you can leave your dog alone. You need not do anything but let the dog work. If however, having sent the dog, you realise he is on a line anywhere to the right of the dummy, then you must be ready to stop your dog before he has gone too far beyond the dummy and re-direct him, bringing him forward on the opposite side so that he will cross the line of the wind and therefore touch the scent. When you see the dog touch the scent then you can leave him alone and let him work.

One last point in terms of reading and understanding your dog: and this point is usually breed related and therefore true of the majority of dogs within a certain breed; and that is the *way* dogs scent.

By this I mean, in simple terms, how high or low the dog holds its' head when hunting and trying to locate the scent of an item.

I am going to generalise here: whilst accepting that there are variations within a breed, it is usual for Labrador retrievers to hold their heads much lower to the ground than say Golden or Flat Coated retrievers. Labradors are frequently referred to as 'ground scenting' and Goldens and Flat Coats referred to as 'air scenting', with Flat Coated retrievers holding their heads much higher than Goldens.

It is important to be aware of these breed characteristics not only to give you opportunities to read your own dog but to learn to see when it touches some scent and be ready to encourage or help in some way to reinforce or discourage the dog as necessary.

Further Control

If you need to see this for yourself, and it is useful to do this, go and watch different dogs and observe how some will hunt with nose to the ground and locate a bird or dummy and how others will touch scent like grabbing a bubble floating a foot or two from the ground and immediately turn into the breeze and move into the scent.

It is amazing how many people are not aware of these breed characteristics which tend to be true of every dog within a breed.

Knowing can help; not knowing can result in dogs being misunderstood and sometimes punished unjustly. There are even judges who do not understand these particular characteristics! Handlers have some excuse until they learn about it, but judges do not, in my opinion; as they should have learnt about it!

I remember being put out of a Field Trial on one occasion by a Field Trial panel judge because my Golden Retriever was not hunting. She was in the right area, in a field of root crops, but after only a short time I was told to call my dog up and put the lead on. I did that, but I must have looked puzzled by this comment because his next words were *'she hadn't got her nose to the ground; she was running with her head up'*.

One obviously cannot argue with judges in these, or any circumstances, but I would have dearly loved to ask him why he was judging an Any Variety Retriever Field Trial when he obviously did not know the characteristics of all the varieties competing.

He was assessing the work and judging all the dogs as Labrador retrievers, despite the fact that they were not!

If my dog had been hunting with her head to the ground she would not have been working properly and would have stood little chance of scenting the wounded bird.

She was doing as she should have been, the only way she knew how, and that was hunting with her head up trying to locate some scent. She was air scenting, the way that most Golden Retrievers do!

Nuala
(Photograph: Anthea Lawrence)

Further Control

CHAPTER FOUR

Alfie
(Photograph: Anthea Lawrence)

Hunting – Training and Exercises

You need to find some training ground which has a small, well defined area of rough grass so that the items such as dummies or balls you will be using will be hidden from view. A corner of a field is ideal for this as you have a triangular area which will have fencing or a hedge on two sides, thus restricting the area a dog can go. This restricted area will help confine dogs which tend to be wide-ranging but will also serve in giving confidence to less bold dogs as the area will be small. You can then proceed as follows:

> ☻ When you get to the training area leave your dog in the car and go alone to place a dummy in the defined area.

You must remember where you have put it, so place it near a distinctive weed or in a spot which you will easily remember. Having placed the dummy go and get the dog and with the dog off the lead at heel, walk with the dog into your area of rough grass. Try and begin when you about 6 feet away from the dummy and as you walk, say 'Hie Lost'. The dog may be a little confused because up to this point he has always seen or heard a mark first.

Keep walking and encouraging, by using your hands if necessary (I use a side-to-side movement of the hand by moving it at the wrist) and hopefully he will find the dummy. You need, when he has found the dummy, to praise him but also make sure you insist on a sit with a good present at the end.

If all has gone well, when you have praised and taken the dummy, walk again and say 'Hie Lost'. There is no other dummy there at this stage, but keep walking and giving the command and encourage the dog to hunt more of the area.

You must make sure that you do not indicate, by any means, that you know there is no other dummy there, so keep everything the same as before.

When he has hunted for a while you need to place a dummy on the ground, but this needs to be done carefully so that the dog does not see or hear you do this. Keep walking and encouraging and walk back towards where you placed the second dummy. Try not to actually stand over it or point the dummy out to the dog, but encourage him to find it by hunting.

Try to keep in mind that this is a hunting exercise. It is not about finding the dummy which, on this occasion, is purely an extra reward for the dog and serves to reinforce the fact that if he hunts efficiently, and on your command, that he succeeds.

When he has successfully found the second dummy don't do any more that session. Go on to do some other training in a different part of the ground and save your defined area to use next time when you will develop this a little further.

Further Control

🐾 The next session, take with you 3 or 4 tennis balls. Leave the dog in the car and go on your own to your defined area. Throw your tennis balls into the area but make sure they are well separated and not on top of each other.

Go and get the dog, and this time stand on the edge of the area, line your dog up to face the centre of the area and give him a *'go back'* command and immediately give a *'hie lost'* command. Hopefully he will remember that last time, in this exact place, he found a dummy, so he will not need too much encouragement.

Encourage as much as necessary and as soon as he finds one of the balls be ready with your whistle to recall him as soon as he has the ball in his mouth. When he has the ball he may just remember too, that he picked a second dummy last time and may go and look for a second ball before coming back to you.

This is not what we want, so you will have to be quick on the recall and if necessary, growl and insist that he comes back to you. You need to be continuing to teach the dog that when he has something in his mouth his job is to come back to you immediately and not go off 'sight seeing'!

After you have praised, and taken the ball from him, line him up again and send him back into the area. Use the same commands of 'go back' then 'hie lost'. He may have to hunt for slightly longer this time, but keep encouraging and again be ready with your whistle to recall as soon as he finds the next ball.

For a dog who is continuing to hunt on the 'hie lost' command I think it is also important to put in some praise occasionally too. You are praising the dog for continuing to obey you out there and it is the praise which will keep him working rather than too many 'hie lost' commands.

When your dog has picked 2 of the tennis balls leave him on a sit, and you should then go and pick up the remaining balls.

This exercise so far, will have shown you that the dog understands the 'hie lost' command, is able to go into an area on a blind at a short distance, will hunt, and will come back to you immediately he has something in his mouth.

It will have shown the dog that you are to be trusted and by hunting he gets his retrieve, but more importantly, he receives your praise, simply by following your commands. It will also prove to him what a marvellous game finder you are because you knew the items were there and he had no idea they were there. Further more, after he picked two, you went on to pick another two all by yourself without the benefit of his superior skills! He will go home thinking he has probably landed in the best pack in the world, with the best leader a dog could ask for!

It is important to continue, in your training sessions, with all other aspects of training taught to the dog so far and you do not need to do these types of exercises every day or every training session.

If there are any problems encountered with other areas of training it is better to deal with these if and when they occur and go back a few steps rather than try to push on into other areas.

Similarly if your dog does not manage these two exercises very well then repeat them, in the same place until he understands what you want. What you want may differ with different types of dogs: if he is a quiet more sensitive dog you need him to begin to work on his own with more confidence; if he is a bold, outgoing dog you may want him to work with perhaps less enthusiasm, and under your control if he wants to go further or not stick to the area where you want him to hunt. When you and the dog are ready for further work on hunting however, you can proceed as follows:

Further Control

> 🐾 Get a friend to come with you to the same area previously used.

You should stand facing the area, but a few yards away rather than on the edge. Have your dog at heel on a sit, off the lead. Your friend should stand on the edge of the area, to the side. Get your friend to shout *'mark'* and throw a dummy or ball into the area.

After the dog has marked the dummy, turn round and walk with the dog several yards away. Your dog should already be used to doing this for 'go back' training, so it will not be new to him.

Whilst you are walking away your friend's job is to pick up the thrown dummy. When this has been accomplished, turn round and walk back towards the area again with your dog at heel. Line the dog up, give him a 'go back' command and when he is in the area, give him the 'hie lost' command.

He should hunt with plenty of enthusiasm, because he thinks the dummy is there. Keep encouraging him with praise and after he has hunted for a while, blow your stop whistle to command your dog to sit. When he does sit, praise him and then recall him to you, with lots of praise when he returns.

The dog should not hunt again after being re-called, so you must insist he returns to you without further hunting. As he is coming back to you, your friend should replace the dummy in the area without the dog hearing or seeing this done.

When the dog is back with you, praise him and then line him up again. Give him a *'go back'* command and a *'hie lost'* when he gets into the area.

This time he may be a little more hesitant because he thinks he has hunted and there is no dummy there, Encourage and hopefully he will find the dummy pretty quickly. Be ready to re-call him, if necessary, once he has found the dummy and give him lots of praise when he returns. The sit and present afterwards should remain perfect.

This exercise will teach the dog several things: firstly, that he must hunt thoroughly. He should be thinking along the lines of, *'I thought I had hunted well, I couldn't find it the first time but the second time I found it so I should have hunted a bit better the first time'.* Next time the dog should hunt a little better and not give up but he will also have much more faith in you because you have shown him that you have superior skills in knowing the dummy was there. You are therefore a good leader for whom he will have respect.

There is no point in doing this exercise again, do it once only, leave him to figure it all out!

Further developments.

Once you have completed these three exercises you will need to try different but relatively simple hunting exercises in other places so the dog understands that hunting is hunting and is not confined to a particular area. Build up gradually and keep the exercises fairly simple other than the fact that they are in different places, using different terrain and features and also using different items to find, which will keep the dog's interest.

Now is the time when you can introduce a different and new command to the dog if you wish and that is *'Get In'*. I use this command to indicate to the dog that I want him to get into or at least get his head and nose into a dense bush or patch of rough grass or anything which may be hiding a wounded bird. It is quite a useful command on occasions when perhaps you have seen a runner disappearing into a patch of brambles but the dog has not.

Further Control

On some days the scent may be sufficient to draw the dog in. On other days the scent may be bad and the dog will run all round the patch but not get his nose into where he may pick up scent.

Once the dog learns what the words mean, he will enter such areas on command when necessary. It is one of the commands which may not be used very often, because once your dog is hunting at a distance from you, most dogs will locate dummies and birds without this type of help being necessary. It is useful on the occasions mentioned however, and to be able to use it to advantage occasionally in the future, you need to practice with the dog and make sure he understands that he *physically* gets himself into these small but rough areas.

These occasions are frequently the ones whereby the dog has run round the bush, picked up no scent and therefore, as far as he is concerned, decided that the bird is not there and he therefore goes off somewhere else. It is an occasion where you will be effectively saying to the dog, *'there may not be scent where you have been, but I want you to go in further, where I know there may be scent.'*

The dog will only begin to trust this occasional command, if you condition him at this stage to obey the command, but most importantly, that when practicing he actually finds something, having obeyed you. Use it carefully therefore and make sure that having got your dog into a rough area that you have put a dummy in first or even better, put some cold game in there. In this way the dog is more likely to understand, and carry out your wishes.

When practicing, you need to make sure you are close by the bush, or whatever small feature you are using, with the dog. It is often useful to have a stick with you which you can use to part some branches to encourage the dog into the area further.

You need to be careful a young dog does not hurt himself so choose the site with care and set it up so that the dog goes partway in with your help and encouragement, and then hits the scent of whatever you have placed there. In that way the scent of the item will draw him in whilst you give the *'get in'* command. Think of the wind! Try and get the wind or breeze coming off the item towards the dog and you will have success. You must also be careful at the start, not to put a young dog into thick Bramble, thistles or nettles which would hurt him. Eventually he will have to do these things but at this stage, anything which hurts or frightens him will act as a deterrent and what he needs is a positive experience to reinforce the learning and meaning of the command.

Other ideas to incorporate into hunting experience are as follows:

> 🐾 Try walking with your dog, encouraging him to hunt bushes, reeds, hedge lines or anything you can find.

Encourage him to hunt fairly close to you but in the places you indicate. Remember he needs to succeed, so to begin you should make sure there are lots of tennis balls and dummies available, either one or two in each location where you want the dog to hunt.

Sometimes you will need to put dummies out before hand and other times place a dummy when he isn't looking. On subsequent sessions you can decrease the number of items you put out so you would expect him to hunt on occasions when there is nothing there. You must reward the dog with praise however and it is important to remember the praise is for hunting, not for finding something although praise must also be given for this too!

Gradually extend the time you expect him to hunt before he finds something but never let him hunt for a long time without finding. You need to read your own dog and reward him with finding something if he is inclined to slow down or get discouraged or alternatively make him hunt for longer before finding something if he is a more outgoing and bold dog.

Further Control

> 🐾 Try getting a friend to put a few dummies in a wood, send your dog in and get him hunting on his own.

Find an area where you are unable to see the dog and find out if he is able to do the job without you by his side or in sight. It is better if your friend can stay just inside the wood to watch the dog and let you know when he has found a dummy so you can recall him.

It is also useful for someone to watch your dog when he knows you cannot see him. Some dogs go to pieces and think they cannot possibly work all on their own; some dogs forget the task they should be doing and go off sight-seeing; other dogs get on with the job but may try to bring back more than one dummy at a time.

A friend in the wood can help in alerting you to any problems, so you can then go to deal with anything necessary. This is all useful information for you and will indicate on which areas you may have to do some additional work as appropriate.

> 🐾 Find a strip of land which has a well-defined boundary or geographical features which will allow you to define an area in your own mind. You can then start some hunting with the dog when you allow him to be further away from you but where you remain in control of the situation.

This is usually called 'Quartering' in gundog language and is more a feature of breeds such as those contained within the Hunt, Point and Retrieve group and Spaniels. However it is a useful add-on for retrievers although some appear much more able to do this effectively than others.

The situation where it is particularly useful is when 'sweeping up'. This is a term used by handlers employed as Pickers-up on a shoot.

When a drive is finished there are occasions where one or more handlers and dogs go to certain sections of land where birds may have fallen. It is better, if circumstances allow it, to perform this operation in a systematic way in order to ensure all of the area has been covered. If dogs are just sent into a wood, for example, and a handler stays outside the wood, there is no guarantee that all the dead and wounded birds will have been retrieved.

If however, one or more handlers and dogs start inside the wood, and walk slowly through in a straight line with the dog or dogs in front covering the ground from side to side, it is more likely that birds will not be missed.

> 🐾 Start first by defining an area for yourself. Go on your own without the dog and make sure you have a good understanding of your defined area. Then throw out a selection of dummies and balls in different places and count how many you are placing.

You can do this if you are working on your own but, better still, is if you can find a friend to place items in the area for you. In this way you will not know where items are and you can work in a much better way to cover the entire area and ensure against working your dog to and for a specific item because you know it is there.

On a shoot day you would not know where birds may be. It is also of benefit in terms of your dog finding items, with scent on them, which is not yours.

You can then go and get the dog. You need to keep the defined area in mind all the time and be ready, if your dog gets to the boundary, to stop him and turn him back into the defined area. You should walk slowly in a straight line. The dog should move from side to side of you, a short distance in front and when he gets to the edge of your defined

Further Control

area you will need to blow your stop whistle and then give a hand signal left or right, to bring him back into the area.

If you see a dummy when walking on your straight line, pick it up yourself. This is what you would do on a shoot day.

Your dog will hopefully start to find, and bring back to you, dummies he has found. When taking these from him, all other aspects of his training concerning steadiness and presentation should remain the same. You should then send the dog from you as you did when beginning and encourage him to hunt again.

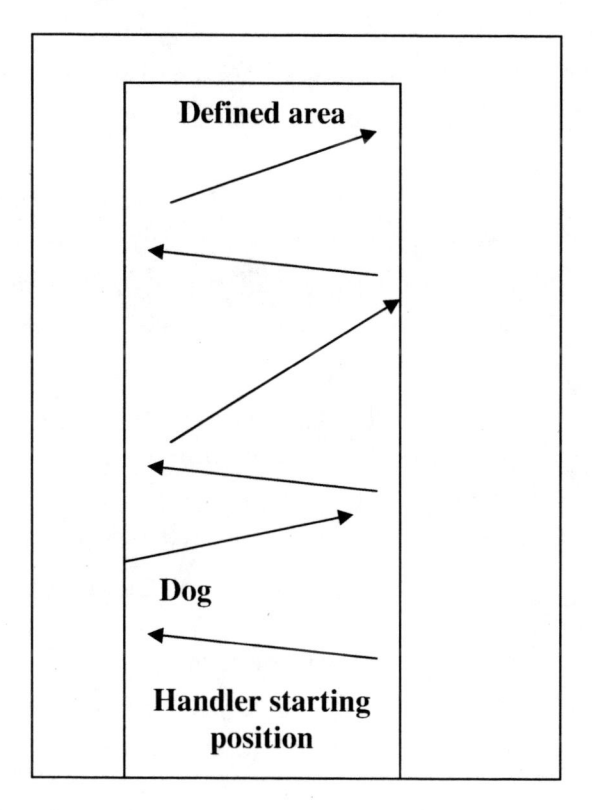

Diagram showing a defined area with a zig-zag path indicating the dog's hunting pattern, starting from the Handler starting position at the bottom.

Don't let the dog get too far away but use your whistle to give one toot to get him looking at you, then use your arms and give a *'get on'* command or use the recall whistle.

Praise him for hunting, praise for everything he does correctly and get him really keen on searching every part of an area. The idea with this type of hunting is to keep the dog on the move so, although you will be using the stop whistle to ensure the dog looks at you, the subsequent commands should follow very quickly to ensure the whole process is free-flowing and that all the area is covered.

With fairly sensitive dogs, keeping them moving is perhaps more necessary but with bolder dogs it may be better to build in a certain amount of waiting after the stop whistle to ensure the dog does as commanded and does not disappear over the far horizon leaving you to the search the area on your own!

> 😊 This exercise can be developed further by having two or three handlers with dogs working a defined area.

Start with perhaps only one other handler and dog and build up gradually. This helps the dogs understand that they are still controlled by their own handler and to learn to distinguish whistle commands meant for them, as opposed to those meant for another dog. Young dogs can also get used to the idea that they are not out for a 'jolly' and they should be stopped from playing with each other. Playing is natural and often occurs the first few occasions that dogs are in a hunting situation and working alongside other dogs. They soon get used to working on their own and not interfering with others, but handlers must be vigilant.

Another problem which can emerge at this time is that of one dog trying to take a dummy away from a dog which has found one and is taking it back to the handler. You need to try and stop this happening and this is easier if you keep your dog close to you, and in view, so you can step in and deal with it if necessary. You should also be aware that this is an occasion where your dog may be tempted to swap dummies and again you should be close to your dog and deal with this promptly. (See Chapter Thirteen)

Further Control

As you continue with all aspects of training you will find numerous places where you can increase the experience for your dog on hunting exercises and where you can broaden his understanding of hunting. Try hunting by water, on the banks, just into the water, hidden in reeds; try every situation you can find which will increase the dog's expertise and skills and help him develop his nose. Find different types of ground and areas where the scent of the vegetation is different for example heather, root crops, kale, long grass, boggy land - *anything and everything!*

Remember to keep control! Some dogs go a bit wild when allowed to hunt too much. Never let the dog go beyond a set distance before making contact with him and don't be afraid to recall the dog and make him come back to you on occasions. Coming back to you is just as important as the hunting, even when the dog has not found something.

Never let the dog believe that he only comes back when he has something in his mouth. He comes back because you have told him to, otherwise he is in **BIG** trouble! If you have a dog reluctant to recall when he is hunting and before he has found something you will need to put a recall in every so often. Insist on obedience but, of more importance, this type of dog needs excessive praise when he returns to you and with a hunting fanatic it would be wise to keep the dog with you at heel every so often after a hunt and recall. Make it so that the heelwork must be perfect, otherwise the dog does not go hunting again in that session.

All dogs need praise when obeying the recall whistle or any other command, but the praise needs to be adjusted according to the level of effort required by the dog to obey and in this way all dogs should then return quickly and on the first command given.

For dogs who have been reluctant to hunt or *prefer* returning to you rather than to keep working at a distance, recalls should be less frequent and the praise for hunting and continuing to work at a distance, should be increased so that the dog understands he is doing the right thing and by so doing, gets his praise *out there*.

If this type of dog keeps returning to you without being called, do not praise excessively, in fact you do not need to praise at all. You don't need to be cross either but simply send the dog back out to hunt and *then* give excessive praise. Timing is crucial and you need to make sure that you praise whilst the dog is engaged in hunting, because this is what you are asking the dog to do.

Vary the way you send a dog out to hunt an area on occasions; leave the dog close to the area and you move away and then send him back, leave the dog sideways on to the area you move away and give him a *'get on'*. This way, although the dog is stationary, you are handling him from a greater distance and also giving the dog plenty of varied experience on the use of all the commands.

Very often at this stage of training when multiple dummies or tennis balls are being used, you may come across a problem not encountered before and that is of the dog swapping dummies.

You will have been incorporating the message, into the ethics of retrieving for the dog, that *'when you have found something and you have it in your mouth, your job is to come straight back to me'*.

Most situations however have not given a dog a retrieving choice or involved more than one dummy, other than when the dummies were quite a distance apart. Many situations also have been set up so that a dog was visible and if necessary you were able to put a recall command in once you have seen that the dog had the dummy in his mouth.

Many dogs understand that they find something, pick it up, take it back to the handler and ignore anything else seen or scented. Some, however, do not!

Further Control

As with most things, handlers need to be aware of what their dog is doing and also be aware of what the dog *may* do.

This is all part of reading your own particular dog but also being aware of the circumstances. If you know there are multiple dummies or other articles in an area you must also bear in mind that your dog may see or scent something else. When the dog has already found a dummy, picked it up, and is on his way back to you, if he scents something, he may well be tempted to go and investigate.

Preventing the dog from swapping is preferable to allowing the dog to swap and then thinking *'oh dear, my dog put that dummy down, picked up another one and brought that one instead'*. With some dogs this could even reach the levels of a dog finding 6 different articles, swapping each in favour of the next one found, having a great time doing it and the handler doing nothing but wringing their hands and looking worried!

This type of behaviour by a dog is a nightmare on a shoot as you and others can never be certain where the birds are. Also, some dogs will not pick up game if another dog has had it in its mouth. If you are beside the dog, you could insist, but you may not be close and would not realise that the dog had rejected a bird.

I will suggest ways of trying to solve this problem (see Chapter Thirteen), but remember prevention is easier than cure, so be aware!

In case anyone is wondering what is wrong with a dog swapping one item in favour of another, I will explain.

First of all we must remember that we are training dogs to work with us on the shooting field.

For any dog engaged in the job of retrieving birds, the dog's job is to bring back each bird to his handler as quickly as possible so that the handler can deal with the retrieved item of game. That will mean either:

place the bird safely in a game carrier to protect it prior to being hung on the game cart; or dispatch wounded birds as quickly as possible, to avoid suffering, before placing the bird in the game carrier.

No-one knows when they send a dog to retrieve a shot bird, whether that particular bird is actually dead. Some wounded birds may stay in one place after being shot and landing on the ground. They may look dead but are not. Some birds recover slightly when they reach the ground but can run later.

If a dog retrieves one bird, finds another and puts the first bird down, the bird he puts down may run off and be lost forever because wounded birds will hide or a duck will dive under the water. This means a bird lost which cannot be counted for the day's bag and one bird lost could mean the loss of £30 or more to the shoot owner or keeper. More importantly however, it means that birds will then be left to die a lingering and unnecessarily painful death or be caught and eaten later by a fox. A dog which persistently swaps birds in this way is not an asset to any shoot and this type of behaviour brings shooting itself into disrepute.

Shooting is a means of providing food for human consumption, and this should always be remembered when working your dogs. It is for this reason that dogs who are hard-mouthed (bite and damage birds, thus making the bird unsuitable to eat) are not welcome on shoots and dogs which pick up birds, drop them, pick up another and drop that one, are also not welcome.

This aspect of a dog's education is an important factor which needs to be addressed at some point with most dogs. You should not wait until your dog is working on live game to find that he has developed this habit or realise that he has always had this habit but you did nothing about it!

Further Control

Once your dog is hunting well, understands what he is to do and what he is not to do and, most importantly, is on the whistle; some dogging-in may be a useful way of furthering aspects of hunting and many keepers will be happy for you to do this in most months of the late summer and between shoots in season.

**Alfie
(Photograph: Anthea Lawrence)**

Hunting and Dogging-In

Seamus (Cocker Spaniel) and Gemma (Golden Retriever)
Dogging-in.
(Photograph: Mary Ward)

- Dogging-in, in the late summer is a help to the keeper and a useful way for young dogs to understand: hunting; the principles of ignoring rabbits and young pheasants when they have *'gone away'*; learning about responses to the stop and recall whistles; and obeying other commands such as a 'get-over' shown here on a deep and fast flowing river.

It is also great fun for the dogs and an extremely useful situation for a handler to discover whether their dog will obey them despite the excitement of the situation and of the scents available.

Further Control

Handler dealing with retrieved birds

When sweeping-up after a drive, the dog's job is to bring back each bird he finds to the handler. The handler then deals with the bird by either dispatching it, as speedily as possible, or by placing it in a game carrier prior to putting it onto the game cart. The dog should not interfere with this, once he has presented the bird to hand, but should simply wait, under control until told what to do next.

(Photograph: David Tomlinson)

CHAPTER FIVE

Gemma
(Photograph: Anthea Lawrence)

Double retrieves, Diversions and Distractions

A double retrieve is, as the name suggests, a situation whereby your dog will have two retrieves to accomplish in one exercise. In case anyone is in any doubt about this, it is not a situation where your dog would be expected to pick two birds or dummies *at the same time*. As with all other aspects of training, as soon as your dog has something in his mouth, his job is to return to you, and bring the dummy or bird back immediately. A gundog is never expected ever, to collect two items and bring both back to the handler together. If two retrieves are required the handler, once the first retrieve is accomplished, will send the dog to retrieve the second item.

On a shoot this situation will occur if, for example you are picking up behind a gun and he hits 2 birds in rapid succession. Both birds may be wounded, both birds may appear to be dead or one bird may be wounded and the other dead; you may have seen the fall of one or both birds or you may not; the dog may have seen the fall of one or both

Further Control

birds or he may not. Whatever the situation, when you will be sending the dog for both birds in quick succession, this is a double retrieve.

Exercises involving a double retrieve may frequently be encountered in a Gundog Working Test but the situation would not normally apply in a Field Trial. In a Field Trial, even if 2 birds were shot, the handler first in line for a retrieve would be instructed by the judge to send their dog to retrieve one bird and when that bird had been picked, the handler who was next in line would send their dog for the second bird. (See the current Kennel Club *Field Trial Rules & Regulations* for further information on these, and other aspects).

In a Gundog Working Test the double retrieve can consist of the following: 2 marks, 2 blinds, 1 mark and 1 blind or 1 mark and 1 memory. The term 'memory' can mean any of the following:

- That a mark is thrown, and when a dog is returning to the handler with the dummy, another dummy is placed in approximately the same place without the dog seeing or hearing it placed. The dog then has to be sent for the second dummy. This is often used primarily in puppy tests, but could be used at any level. The actual exercise will technically be one mark and one blind but the fact that the blind is placed in the same place as where the marked dummy fell, means that this is a memory test in terms of the dog remembering and returning to the same place.

- The term can sometimes be used in conjunction with what is actually a double mark and some judges will call the second dummy to be thrown in a different place, a memory retrieve. This is because the dog will be sent to retrieve the first dummy thrown and has to remember where the second dummy landed so that when he has retrieved the first dummy, he can be sent for the second without any subsequent handling following the initial command. A similar situation can be where the dog will see the second dummy being thrown a second or two after he has retrieved the first one, whilst returning to the handler. This then is a memory test for the dog remembering he saw a dummy being thrown as well as remembering where it is located.

🐾 Similarly to the above double marked retrieve, which may be encountered in training and Gundog Working Tests, the situation may also apply in a Field Trial. It will not be called a 'memory' but the situation could arise if, for example, 2 birds are shot and something happens before a dog is sent to retrieve. A judge could move one or two handlers so they are in a better position to send their dogs to retrieve a bird or, after birds have been shot and fallen, there may be a delay whilst judges decide which handler should send their dog. After any of these situations or whilst judges are deliberating, both handler and dog need to keep in mind the position of the fallen birds because they do not know which bird they may be told to send their dog to retrieve.

Double retrieves could be on land or water or a combination of both. There may be gunshot to accompany both, neither or just one of the retrieves. The higher the level of Test and age or ability of the dogs entered, the more difficulty there will be in terms of the level of control and training expected of the dog and handler as well as greater distances and differences in terrain.

In a Gundog Working Test, a dog is expected to complete both retrieves in order to gain any points and failure on one retrieve would result in zero points for the whole exercise. (See the current Kennel Club *Field Trial Rules & Regulations* for further information on these, and other aspects as rules may change from year to year).

A diversion or distraction means that something happens, which will attract the attention of the dog. Both words mean the same and strictly

Further Control

speaking a distraction or diversion, in my view, if this is a dummy, should never be retrieved by the dog.

In some Gundog Working Tests people sometimes, use the word 'distraction' or 'diversion' inappropriately or they use it without being explicit in their definition of the word. A dummy will be used as the distraction and the dog will be asked to retrieve the item used in this way, *after* he has retrieved the main object of the exercise, which is another dummy placed or thrown elsewhere.

If the dog is to pick the distraction item, then in my view the exercise is in fact a double retrieve.

I personally do not like the term distraction or diversion unless it is used to mean it is *only* a distraction or diversion. If a dummy has been used, then it should not be part of the exercise for the distraction dummy to be retrieved by the dog.

Frequently, the distraction is not a dummy but simply a shot or the sound of a splash close by but in a direction away from the direction in which the dog will be sent.

The following will assume that distraction or diversion means an exercise when only one item will be retrieved, and that item will not be the one termed the *distraction* or *diversion*.

In terms of the exercise and handling, whatever the distraction is, the dog's attention must be taken from that onto something else. The 'something else' will be the task which the dog must accomplish instead of wanting to go and investigate whatever the distraction is.

That may sound complicated but the practical use of training on distractions is that on a shoot for example, when the dog is sitting during a drive: he will notice a dead bird that comes crashing through the trees fairly close to him; he will hear the splash of a dead duck as it falls onto the lake; he will see a bird landing on the grass in front of him.

A dog and handler are a partnership on a shoot and handlers must keep an eye on birds flying towards the guns, birds flying towards themselves and they need to make decisions concerning which birds have been shot, which are dead and which are wounded.

If the dog is focussed on a bird making an exciting noise as it crash lands, dead, nearby, he may not notice another bird which is injured and which the handler has seen. The handler knows that the injured bird should be retrieved as soon as possible and that the dead bird, on which the dog is focussed, can safely be left probably until the drive is over. The handler therefore needs to give the dog a command to bring the dog's attention away from what *he* thinks he will be sent to retrieve (the distraction), which is the exciting one, as far as he is concerned, and the one he wants to get.

The handler, having gained the dogs attention needs then to command the dog with a directional command of 'go back' and get the dog to the area the handler saw the bird fall.

What is not required, is to waste valuable time waiting whilst the dog goes crashing about in the bushes for the dead bird *he* saw or is having a lovely time swimming in the lake whilst the handler fruitlessly blows a recall whistle!

The dog may do no actual harm by doing this, but the responsibility of the handler and dog partnership is to collect the wounded birds first. These birds are the ones which should be dispatched quickly; they should not remain in pain longer than necessary, and everything possible should be done to ensure that they do not run away and then have to die over a long period simply because a dog was not under sufficient control.

Further Control

In a Gundog Working Test, there are a variety of ways these exercises may be set up: a dummy thrown, usually as an exciting mark, but that particular dummy will not be retrieved by the dog. Instead the handler will be expected to turn the dog away from that mark and then handle the dog to retrieve a dummy which the dog will not have seen. There could be a gunshot in a certain direction and the dog has to be sent in the opposite, or another, direction to retrieve a dummy. There could be a dummy thrown with the sound of a splash in water but the dog has to be sent away from the sound to pick another dummy.

Such distractions are used to test steadiness and obedience: whether the dog is on the whistle and listening to its handler; whether it will go on command to where the handler wants him to go, with as little in terms of commands and handling as possible.

Few commands from a handler and total obedience from a dog means less noise from a handler, and a speedier retrieve of a bird. All these things will cause less disruption to a shoot; will not interfere with the guns, birds or other handlers and their dogs. It also means there will be less likelihood of a dog heading off to an inappropriate area where live birds may be. These birds may be required for the next drive and you will not be very popular with the keeper and shoot owner if your dog has already put up all the birds required for later!

The dog should not, for example, ignore the handler, retrieve the distraction or go towards the distraction and then require numerous commands either by whistle or verbal shouts of 'no' or 'leave it' repeatedly, before the dog obeys. In a competition one should never man-handle a dog either, in order to get the dog's attention or to make the dog adopt the desired and correct position.

All these factors are relevant to how it would be on a shoot. A dog which is disobedient and goes, despite the commands of his handler, to do what *he* wants to do is not an asset and he is in fact a liability and could disrupt the whole shoot. In addition the handler will, by necessity, disrupt the shoot in issuing numerous verbal and whistle commands in order to regain control of the dog.

If disruption, by handler, dog or both, happens too often or with disastrous consequences, the partnership may not be invited back another time! We are there to help, not hinder, and must bear in mind that we are very much the 'back-stage' help. It is the guns who pay for the day and they want a pleasant day's shooting without having their concentration broken repeatedly by either noisy handlers or dogs flying around at speed in front of them. They prefer the noise, flying and speed to be from the Pheasants, Ducks or Partridges!

Finally, regarding distractions; it should also be part of your training programme now to introduce some distractions to the dog, not in relation to birds, dummies and shots but in relation to other things going on around them when you are training.

Dogs should be steady around sheep, water fowl, rabbits, horses and any other live-stock which happens to be around. One must be careful, however if you can introduce some aspects of distraction, whilst keeping control of the dog as well as the dog keeping control of itself, it will be extremely useful.

Gemma
(Photograph: Anthea Lawrence)

Further Control

Distractions need to be carefully incorporated into situations where you train your dog.

Here, Canada Geese and Mallards with goslings and ducklings, can provide ideal distractions for dogs when doing some basic obedience exercises

(Photographs: Anthea Lawrence)

A training class taking place with deer roaming, just yards away, from handlers and dogs waiting for their next exercise.

(Photographs: Mary Ward)

Further Control

CHAPTER SIX

Alfie and Tiggy
(Photograph: Anthea Lawrence)

Double retrieves – Training and Exercises

<u>The double mark.</u>

To begin training a dog for a double retrieve, it is best to start on two marks. At this stage of training, your dog should hopefully, be steady and will wait before being given a name command, at which point he should go speedily, and to the exact fall of one marked dummy, bringing it to you with a good present and with no problems in any areas.

If there are any problems at all, these should be addressed as appropriate, and under no circumstances should you begin to train your dog on double marks or any other combination of double retrieves. If your dog cannot retrieve one mark properly, then there is no reason to believe he will be able to do two! In fact if your dog cannot retrieve one mark perfectly I can guarantee that if you give him a double mark, each will be worse than the dog's performance on one mark.

In addition, your dog should be able to go away from you in a straight line on a 'go back' command and retrieve a simple blind. By a 'simple blind' I mean in a straight line, perhaps along a track or some geographical feature which runs in a straight line. Your dog should, at this stage be able to go a considerable distance from you with no further commands after the initial one. If your dog cannot retrieve one blind properly, then there is no reason to believe he will be able to do two!

Another point to mention here is that you should never, on a double retrieve say 'leave it' to the dog after he has seen the first or second dummy thrown. First of all there should be no need to say this to your dog at this stage of his training as it was a command used to build up the steadiness aspects which should now be firmly in place.

Secondly, some dogs take this command literally, for ever, and I have known dogs which, having been given a 'leave it' or similar command, will not go anywhere near the dummy when sent on a 'go back' command later in the exercise. The dog is absolutely right to do this as he is being very obedient and if having an obedient dog is your requirement, you cannot pick and choose when you want him to obey and when you want him to disobey!

If your dog will not sit at heel, watch a dummy being thrown and remain steady without you shouting 'leave it' then you have no right to be doing double retrieves. Get the other aspects sorted first then you will not have to shout 'leave it'!

It is not possible to do this type of training on your own. For those who have worked on the training concerning marked retrieves in *'Taking Control'* you will have already ensured that you do not throw marks yourself for your dog to retrieve but will only have sent your dog to retrieve dummies thrown by someone else. A double is no different

Further Control

in this respect so you will need someone, or preferably two other people, to throw dummies for you.

Remember that you are teaching the dog what will be required of him. For you this exercise may seem no different from doing single marks and blinds but to your dog it is totally different so keep it simple and concentrate on the lesson you are trying to teach. Begin by having a mark in front, a short distance away. There is no point in having a mark a huge distance away or making complications in terms of the mark or the fall not being visible; that is not the lesson you should be teaching. Distance and complications can be built in later, once the initial training is completed.

After the mark has been thrown, about-turn on the spot, and give a 'heel' command to the dog, so that he turns too. Give your dog a 'sit' command.

Once you and the dog are in the correct position then get the dummy thrower to throw the second dummy which, again, should be a short distance and visible. Do not be tempted to rush all these steps. This is not only about getting the dummies; it should be mainly about ensuring the dog obeys your commands principally, on these turning and steadiness aspects. You already know your dog will retrieve. What you do not know, and what you are teaching now, is whether the dog, despite having seen one dummy thrown, and then another thrown, will continue to obey commands which to him, may be the opposite of what he thinks they should be.

Now although technically both these dummies are marked retrieves in that you and the dog have seen both dummies thrown and land, they should be treated as though they are blinds. My definition of a mark is: that someone has said 'mark', or there has been a gunshot, or you and the dog have seen the dummy thrown and/or land or heard it land; but in addition, *nothing else has happened* in between seeing the dummy or bird land and then sending the dog.

In this case, something else has happened in between; so, having seen the second dummy thrown, you should about-turn on the spot giving your dog a 'heel' command as you turn and then give the dog a 'sit' command. Take your time over all this as you will gain nothing by rushing. Most of what you have done so far in this exercise is exactly the same as the dog already knows so you must keep control and make sure the dog understands that although parts of the exercise are a little different, everything else must remain the same in terms of obeying you.

Remember that both these dummies need to be treated as a 'go back' so line the dog up correctly with your hand and arm outstretched and pointing at the dummy. Make sure your dog is facing and looking on the correct line and send him for the first dummy with a 'go back' command. When he returns and has presented the dummy to you correctly, praise him and then either do an about-turn to face the second dummy and give your dog a 'heel' command so he faces the same way, or you walk round the dog into the heel position as the dog will already be facing in the correct direction. You should then line the dog up to face the second dummy and send him on a 'go back' command.

I have seen numerous people treat a double mark as if it is exactly the same as one mark multiplied by two and they send their dog on a name command for each. I feel that this practice has risks which I prefer not to take, and that is why I remain committed to my definition of a mark being a situation where you send a dog immediately, from that place, with nothing else happening in between.

The other problem of course, for those determined to send the dog on a name command for each retrieve, is that later developments with double marks will mean that the two dummies may be much closer together. At this stage they are poles apart but you are setting the scene and teaching the dog what he should do for life. People sending their

Further Control

dogs on name command at this stage, frequently have to change their command later when exercises get more complicated, or they change their commands only in a Gundog Working Test situation. I believe this to be unfair on the dog and prefer to teach one rule and stick to that rule. In this way, no matter how complicated things may get in the future, nothing will have to change for the dog or handler.

Imagine the situation where you and the dog see one dummy thrown and land and then you and the dog turn to watch another dummy being thrown and land: if you were then to send the dog for the *last* dummy thrown, then you could send the dog on a name command as this would be a mark in the full meaning of the definition. If however you see one dummy thrown, turn round to see another dummy thrown, and you are to send the dog for the *first* dummy thrown then you and the dog have to turn round again before you send the dog. This means that something else *has* happened in between and you should not therefore use the name command but use the 'go back' command for both dummies.

In this situation you should only use the 'go back' command for each retrieve because although they are 'marks' they are not marks where you will be sending the dog immediately. You need to be very careful in this situation to make sure you do not use the dog's name inadvertently.

Many handlers have problems with this and usually these are because handlers have developed a bad habit of using their dog's name too frequently. Consequently one sees handlers and dogs watch both dummies thrown; the dog is perfectly steady and attentive and then the handler makes a fatal error by saying *'Copper, Heel'*.

'Copper' is the dog's name as well as his command to go and retrieve a marked dummy, and he has just seen the last marked dummy thrown, so what does the dog do? Well, he goes and does what he has been trained to do; he is an obedient dog, he wants to please his pack leader, he wants to go and get the dummy, so he goes as soon as he hears the command and is long gone before the next command of 'heel'. He therefore goes, finds the dummy and brings it back to give to his leader at speed. Brilliant, clever dog!

Unfortunately, he will not be seen as a clever dog by his handler. He will be seen as disobedient, wilful, and numerous other negative words which will be accompanied by shouting, loud whistle commands, lead being put on, and being dragged off in disgrace. What on earth is the dog to make of all this? He has done exactly what he has been taught to do; he has done it stylishly and perfectly and yet, instead of being praised he has been punished.

A bold out-going dog may be able to cope with this behaviour from his inconsiderate handler. A sensitive dog may well have problems in understanding, and who could blame him? Fortunately many handlers learn from this but unfortunately, some handlers do not!

This situation is total handler error and not the fault of the dog!

<u>The steps for a double mark are as follows:</u>
- Handler with dog off lead, at heel on a sit.
- One dummy is thrown in front.
- Handler and dog to about-turn.
- The second dummy is thrown
- Handler and dog to about-turn
- Handler sends dog on a 'go back' command for the first dummy.
- After the present, handler and dog to about-turn.
- Handler sends dog on a 'go back' command for the second dummy.

If you take your time, insist on your dog being in the correct position at all times when he is with you, this exercise should be accomplished with little difficulty.

Further Control

<u>Problems.</u>

If there are any problems, I can guarantee that they are unrelated to doing a double mark and as such, need to be worked on as separate training issues.

The solution to a problem never lies at the point where the problem is perceived so the first thing to do is to stop attempting the double mark at whatever point the problem is displayed. Stop immediately, pick up the dummies and work out what to do. The most common problem for many handlers is that they have done insufficient work with the dog, particularly in making sure the 'heel' and 'sit' commands are obeyed *no matter what!*

This then creates steadiness problems, amongst others, but for this particular exercise this is shown by a dog which marks the first dummy and then will not turn on the 'heel' command. Some dogs may run-in at this point in which case, you should make sure the dummy thrower picks the dummy up before the dog can get to it.

You should follow the dog but not give a command. Growl at him, put the lead on and take him back to the exact spot you were both on, at the time he ran-in. You do not need to shout at the dog; you do not need to blast the whistle in his ear; you do not need to do anything other than quietly put the lead on the dog and walk back with him, with no command, no conversation, to the starting point. Your silence alone will indicate to the dog that he has done something wrong. Silence speaks much louder than words in these instances!

You need to keep the dog focussed on the issue regarding his disobedience and it is very important not to give any command whilst you are taking the dog back to the point where he disobeyed. If you give any kind of command or speak it will take his mind off the point in question but as well, if he obeys your subsequent command(s) you will have to praise him at a time when you don't really want to praise him because you are in the middle of sorting out the first problem.

The first problem has to be addressed by putting him back where he should have been. I do not believe that this 'putting back' needs, or should, be done in any kind of rough manner.

Doing it roughly, harshly in some cases, was the way it used to be done, the way I was taught, but it does not work any better than doing it *without* inflicting some kind of physical pain on the dog - it in fact can make the situation worse. Harsh treatment can block out much of what has gone before and a dog cannot remember what he did wrong. If the dog cannot remember, the punishment is worthless and the training opportunity is lost. Training should not be about how to punish it should be about *'how can I teach my dog what he needs to learn?'*

The growl, lead on and going back with you to the exact spot, in silence, will tell the dog all he needs to know about the fact that he has done wrong. Perhaps more importantly; doing it calmly keeps the blood pressure of the handler at a reasonable rate, prevents the handler getting cross and actually prevents some handlers inflicting physical pain on the dog which is totally unjustified, I believe as a teaching method.

It is often the handler who gets cross and therefore starts doing and saying all sorts of things which are inappropriate and none of this will teach the dog what he should have done. The handler must remain controlled, remain in control. Silence, in this instance, is truly more golden than speech!

When you and the dog are back on the spot, *then* give him a sit command, and praise him for obeying, take a deep breath, take the lead off the dog, abandon the exercise but do not abandon the training session. Immediately do some steadiness exercises, throwing dummies, doing heelwork through dummies, passing dummies, doing about turns,

Further Control

anything which will reinforce the fact that you must be obeyed under all circumstances, *no matter what.*

If necessary go back to using the 'leave it' command when doing steadiness exercises where the dog will not be required to retrieve anything he sees thrown or which is lying around on the grass.

Then, you must give the dog, by trying the exercise again, the opportunity to put his new understanding into practice. He may not do it perfectly but you must give him the opportunity.

Other dogs will just remain transfixed on the first dummy. They may not run-in but they may refuse to turn.

If the dog is given the heel command, (remember this should be given once only) but disobeys this command, then you should growl at the dog and put his lead on. At the same time get the dummy thrower to pick up the dummy.

Give another heel command to the dog, about turn, and make him obey by using the lead this time. Once you and the dog have done the about turn, *praise the dog.* It is vital to praise the dog when he does obey you: yes, even though you are probably cross and even though you have had to put a lead on him. It is the praise that confirms for the dog that *'yes, what I am showing you, is what I want you to do'.*

Next give a sit command, praise for obeying, and abandon the exercise but do not abandon the training session as you will need to do some appropriate work on basics to reinforce the fact that 'heel' means 'heel' and 'sit' means 'sit'! Practice some swift about turns with the lead and then without the lead. Practice an about turn when a dummy has been thrown. Practice anything along the same theme to show the dog what you want.

Then, you must give the dog, by trying the exercise again, the opportunity to put his new understanding into practice. He may not do it perfectly but you must give him the opportunity.

Another problem which could occur is that a dog may watch both dummies thrown; he will turn on the heel command, and do everything perfectly up to the point where he is returning with the first dummy.

It is at this point that some dogs remember and may want to go immediately to pick the second dummy before delivering the first, appropriately to the handler.

This is not necessarily a huge problem but it can become a problem if the handler fails to be aware that this is likely to happen.

Some handlers relax when, because everything has been perfect up to that point, they send the dog for the first dummy. They forget therefore to concentrate and keep control of the dog, and forget to give the sit command on the recall.

If the dog is obedient, he should obey the recall whistle; he should obey the sit command and also remember how he has been taught to present the dummy.

If all these things are kept in the control of the handler, the dog cannot go to get the second dummy prematurely. You need therefore to examine whether there was handler error in the exercise or whether the handler did everything appropriately but the dog disobeyed.

If the dog did disobey, then these areas of obedience, or disobedience really, should be addressed separately before attempting any other doubles.

If the handler was at fault then you should give yourself a telling off, or rely on someone watching you to point out the error of your ways!

Further Control

Then, you should sort it out in your own mind and make sure you get it right next time, and for every time in the future.

Any of these problems should alert you as to where more training needs to be given.

Look again at all the basics which should be in place and do some appropriate exercise to rectify the problems and positively reinforce the areas of obedience you want. It may take a few minutes or several weeks before you should try this exercise again. It is important to put in any remedial work necessary otherwise, if you continue attempting double marks and your dog continues to disobey, you will only be reinforcing the problems and that will make them worse. Nip it in the bud, and all will be well – eventually!

<u>A mark and a blind.</u>

Once your dog will do a double mark correctly with no steadiness or obedience problems and will retrieve both dummies on command with a good present it will be time to try another type of double but this time with a mark and a blind.

Most of this exercise is exactly the same as when doing a double mark other than one dummy will not be thrown and therefore will not be seen by the dog.

Stand with your dog at heel on a sit, off lead. A dummy should be placed behind you and the dog in a straight line, a short distance away, making sure the dog does not see or hear the dummy being placed. A mark should then be thrown in front. You should then do an about turn with the dog at heel, line the dog up and send him with a 'go back' command, for the blind. Once that dummy is retrieved correctly then about turn with the dog, line the dog up and send him on a 'go back' command for the mark.

Both these dummies should again be treated as though they were both blinds and the 'go back' command used for both.

Provided that you have been diligent in the training concerning the double mark, this exercise should work with no problems because the majority of the exercise has already been learnt by the dog.

If there are any problems, these should be addressed according to the type of problem encountered. Do not try and sort out the problem using the double retrieve exercise, but sort it out by using an appropriate heelwork, steadiness or go back exercise according to the problem encountered.

Double blind.

Once the above two doubles are working satisfactorily it will be time to take things a stage further and try two blinds. Again most of the training has already been achieved for this. The only different aspect of this is that neither of the two dummies will be thrown and therefore neither will be seen by the dog.

Start in exactly the same way as for the other doubles exercises with your dog at heel on a sit facing a dummy which has been placed previously in a straight line. Another dummy should also have been placed in a straight line behind you. Line the dog up to face the dummy and send him on a 'go back' command, for the first dummy. When that one is retrieved correctly, do an about turn and send the dog on a 'go back' command for the second dummy.

This exercise is often easier to complete than previous types of double in that because neither dummy is seen by the dog initially, he has to rely on the handler to tell him what to do. This of course should be the situation always, but many dogs start thinking they know what to do and consequently some only half listen to their instructions when they have seen a dummy.

Further Control

For more hesitant dogs however, going twice into the unknown for two blinds, may well be a little daunting in which case, dummies should be placed much closer to your starting point.

Later, distances can be increased but it is always best, when starting any new exercise, to make distances short and keep in mind the whole purpose of any exercise, which in this case is to teach your dog to go away from you once, find a dummy and then go away from you again and find another dummy, neither of which he has seen. He therefore has to go on trust and obedience to your commands.

<u>A mark and a memory (A mark and a blind in the same place)</u>

To begin this exercise, which is the same as those practiced with young puppies when first beginning 'blind' retrieves, have a mark thrown in front.

This dummy should be retrieved by the dog on a 'name' command. Once the dog has picked this dummy, your dummy thrower should place another dummy in the same place when the dog is returning to you. This should be done without the dog seeing or hearing the dummy being thrown.

Once the dog has successfully retrieved the first dummy, he should be sent back to the same place using a 'go back' command from your side. This is an exercise where the 'memory' part is the dog remembering where he has just been, and where he found a dummy. Actually it is for the handler to remember too and is good handler training in terms of memory and training yourself to link any features around, with the place of the dummy, so that if your position has changed slightly you can remember where the second dummy will be.

Any exercise like this should be used by handlers to improve their own marking ability and we need to train ourselves in this by remembering flowers, fencing or any feature by which we can guarantee we know exactly the spot where we should send the dog.

Many handlers who do not do this correctly, frequently send their dog for the second dummy, on totally the wrong line simply because they have moved their position during the time the dog was retrieving the first dummy, or they didn't bother to remember where the first dummy was thrown, or they forgot to take account of the wind direction.

These things, ideally, should never happen but in particular they should not happen when you are trying to teach a dog something new. The dog must succeed when he obeys your commands and if your commands are inappropriate to the situation the dog will not learn the lesson you are trying to teach.

Much of the early training concerned teaching your dog what he should do to obey your basic commands. Although advanced training is still to improve learning for the dog it is mainly to help the dog's experience of the commands being used in different combinations and in different circumstances. The commands are not being taught, as these have already been learnt, but the circumstances the commands apply are being taught and learnt by the dog.

Advanced training is therefore advancing the knowledge and skills of the dog but more than this, training now is concerned much more with the handler. The handler must have control over themselves in order to take *Further Control* of the dog. Their handling skills should have become second nature and appropriate commands given to the dog without a great deal of thought as the skills, techniques and knowledge grows.

Further developments on all these exercises can now begin to incorporate different distances, different terrain and narrowing angles between the dummies to be retrieved, in order to build up confidence

Further Control

but also to allow the dog to experience as many different situations involving double retrieves as possible.

As with all training matters it is important to build up gradually and enable the dog to succeed.

The following ideas will help to develop this:

- 🐾 Build up distances whereby your dog will have to go away from you further on one command, to retrieve the dummies.

- 🐾 Begin to change and narrow angles so that instead of doing a full about turn, begin with a half turn to the left or right and then a quarter turn.

- 🐾 Develop the dog's understanding of going along the exact line you want by standing whilst two dummies are thrown in front but in a V-shaped formation so that you send the dog slightly left and then slightly right of where you are standing. It is important always to use 'go back' commands to prevent your dog going for an incorrect dummy and to try to ensure he always goes for the dummy required. In training always make sure that if anything goes wrong, someone can pick up a dummy before the dog gets to it. You can then recall the dog and start again so that the dog understands what you want and therefore what he must do.

- 🐾 It is important to try and avoid excessive handling in these exercises particularly when training so aim to have dummies, on any kind of double retrieve, in straight lines. In this way your dog will learn to go further, on a direct line without you having to stop the dog and redirect him at a distance. Aim to get to the point whereby your dog will go on a straight line, in exactly the direction you want, on one command, to further distances before he finds the dummy.

🐾 In building distance into doubles you will also be increasing the time your dog will have to remember where a second dummy has been thrown and therefore increase his memory. When having a long-distance first mark, for example, and then another long-distance second mark, you need to begin to expect the dog will go for the second mark with speed rather than go slowly because he hasn't a clue where it is, as he has forgotten.

🐾 Try to vary the order in which you send a dog for double marks so that you are not inadvertently teaching the dog that he will always be sent for the first dummy thrown. Often this will be the case, but sometimes it is not. As in all matters, the dog should go for the dummy you want but if he is always sent for the first dummy, he will start to believe that this should happen every time and he may start to anticipate, get over keen and perhaps stop listening and watching you to know what he is to do.

It is important too, not to get obsessive about trying to get more and more distance. Vary the lengths so you do not, inadvertently; teach the dog he always has to go 100 yards or 200 hundred yards or whatever.

The dog should pick the dummy from whatever distance the dummy happens to be, so put in a short mark or blind occasionally and keep varying the distances throughout training. It is true that you want the dog to be able to go, for example, 100 yards or 200 yards or more. However impressive that looks, it fades into insignificance if your dog cannot pick up a bird which is 20 yards away simply because he is hell-bent on sprinting 200 yards before he starts looking. A bird 20 yards away, which everyone can see but your dog, apparently, can not, will be the one everyone remembers!

There is no such thing as an easy or difficult retrieve really although some will appear easy or difficult. It is the way each dog and handler partnership approaches the task and the efficiency of how it is effected which will make a complicated retrieve *look* easy and impressive. It

Further Control

could equally make a very easy retrieve look a total shambles from start to finish and look unimpressive apart from the novelty value where most of the guns are standing around laughing at the dog which apparently needs spectacles. Even more embarrassing; having sent your dog to retrieve a near bird and he has disappeared into the far blue yonder, is when one of the guns, after he has finished laughing, walks out a few yards and picks the bird up himself from an open field!

So, the moral of the story, in case you haven't guessed, is vary distances and make sure your dog picks birds and dummies from where they are!

Alfie and Tiggy
(Photograph: Anthea Lawrence)

CHAPTER SEVEN

Bebe
(Photograph: Anthea Lawrence)

Diversions and Distractions – Training and Exercises

As stated previously, the term diversion or distraction is used to indicate something which happens to attract the attention of a dog. The handler must then divert the attention of the dog away from whatever has attracted his attention. Initially the dog must focus his attention back onto the handler and this is accomplished by the handler giving a 'heel' command and turning to move, with the dog, in the direction the dog will be sent. Only when that is accomplished, should the dog be given a command concerning his task. The task for the dog will *never* concern whatever has attracted his attention in the first place!

Much of the training concerning diversion will have already been accomplished in early puppy training: teaching dogs a 'leave it' command; throwing dummies to help a dog in steadiness exercises; teaching a dog the philosophy of remaining in a sit position when commanded, *no matter what* is happening around him or what you or others may be doing; teaching a dog that no matter what has happened or is happening, if you give a command of 'heel' and walk away or turn

Further Control

round, he must come with you; if you give a command of 'sit' then you leave the dog and you walk away and either go straight back, or perhaps pick up a dummy; then all these commands must be obeyed, the command is exactly what a dog must do, immediately he hears the command, no questions asked!

Some of the tools used for this early training, have now been left behind in that you should no longer have to: say 'leave it' to a dog; teach a dog where the heel position is or position a dog when you give a sit command. These were all teaching tools to enable the dog to learn what they should do when they hear a command and as such, they should cease to be used as soon as possible.

I know it is difficult for some people to understand the difference between teaching tools and commands which will remain in place permanently because sometimes, a teaching tool can sound like a permanent command, such as the 'leave it'. If you remember back to the initial teaching of 'leave it', I suggested it was the only exception to the rule that commands should be spoken in a normal voice and that was because 'leave it' is more of a *de*mand than *co*mmand.

It was never designed to remain permanently in place, as a command, in the way that words which *are* commands are kept and used for life.

The way I visualise teaching tools is in thinking about a situation such as having the outside of the house painted. Whilst the work is in progress there are painters, ladders, tins of paint, rollers, trays, bottles of white spirit, scaffolding and white paint-splattered sheets surrounding the house whilst painting is in process.

Once the house has been painted you would not expect all the tools (tins of paint, ladders etc.) to remain in place for ever but you may store a small tin of paint in the shed to use in an emergency.

Think of the 'leave it' command now as the small tin of paint you have stored for emergency use! You should not need to be dipping into it every day! If you do, there is something sadly wrong with the initial job of painting, or in the case of dog training, something wrong with the basic foundations.

The dog will always remember what it means but there should now be very few situations where you use it and it should not be necessary in training. One should also be very careful never to use such a command when, at some point during the same exercise, you may want, or decide, to send the dog for any item for which you have previously applied the 'leave it' command.

The reason for this is that some dogs do that precisely and will not touch the item, come what may and however hard you encourage. I therefore believe it should never be used once the initial basic exercises have been taught to, and learned, by the dog.

If you believe it is necessary, because your dog is not steady, runs in, fails to obey a command when something more exciting is happening, then you should go back to teaching the 'leave it' command and using it to reinforce the message *'dismiss from your mind all thought of having or doing what you are thinking of taking possession of, or getting involved in'* using appropriate basic exercises.

One should never try to reinforce this in the process of teaching complex, more advanced exercises because it is at a basic level where the dog has failed to grasp the message or, where the handler has not taught either correctly or for as long as it takes for the dog to learn. That level is therefore the place to revisit in order to put this particular aspect in place. Once the message is firmly in place then the command should be dropped – for ever, preferably, as it should no longer be required in daily life.

Further Control

I mentioned earlier that the 'leave it' command should be saved and used only in emergencies and for me, the only emergency situation would be, for example, on a shoot with a young dog perhaps in his first full season picking up. If there is a heavy drive in progress and birds are landing left, right and centre but you are simply standing with your dog which is steady, but perhaps showing signs of getting a little agitated by so much activity going on, or when some birds are landing very close to the dog. Then use the command if appropriate.

Often the most appropriate command to reinforce in this situation is the 'sit' command but having done that and then a bird lands, flapping very near by, I would make a quick assessment of the situation and perhaps put in a 'leave it' command also.

It has to be remembered however that it is the 'sit' command which should be obeyed primarily. If the 'sit' command is obeyed and the dog has been well taught that *'sit, means sit, no matter what else may be happening'* then the dog will also be obeying a 'leave it' command, although this should not be necessary to give in reality. The *'leave it'* should now have become part of the dog's self-control – a built-in luxury item that one should now be taking for granted!

If you decided to give the *'leave it'* command, it should only be given when you are then in a position to go and pick the bird up yourself, leaving your dog in a sit, whilst you do it. This would never give the wrong idea to the dog. He will understand it because it was what used to happen when he began his training. If you pick up the bird yourself there will never be a problem where the dog will, subsequently, not retrieve it, because you will never command him to go and retrieve it.

I think it should be used sparingly, if at all; and one should never get into the situation of giving the command for every bird that drops or flaps or runs or for every diversionary dummy. Those who feel the need to give the command are perhaps indicating their own anxiety and if a handler is anxious a dog will detect this very rapidly. So if the handler is standing there thinking *'my dog's going to run in any minute'*, most dogs will oblige!

The danger also, if you get into this habit, is that some dogs see this eventually, as part of their command to remain sitting. Consequently, if you subsequently try and avoid giving the *'leave it'* command, a dog may take this as an invitation to run-in. This is along the lines of *'well, I didn't hear a 'leave it' command, I really want to get that bird, and so I will go'*. This then spoils and disrupts the understanding of sit *means sit, no matter what!'*

So, be very careful and try not to get yourself into a situation which may take months to undo later.

It has been suggested to me in the past that a handler could use a *'leave it'* command in a situation which was a diversion exercise so that the *'leave it'* could be said concerning the diversion. I partly agree, in that as long as one does not want the dummy to be retrieved by the dog it would be a legitimate use of the command. However, I would then need to ask *'why'?*

There must be a problem concerning some other part of a dog's basic training or learning if the *'leave it'* command is needed because otherwise the dog would remain in a sit position. It is this other problem which should be addressed rather than trying to find a way of reducing the risk.

The other danger of course, is that particularly in Gundog Working Tests many people mix up the terms concerning diversions or distractions and double marks and you could get a situation where you are told something like *'There will be a shot fired and a dummy will be thrown into the lake as a diversion. I want you to send your dog down the side of the lake to the reeds at the bottom to retrieve a blind.'*

So you stand whilst your dog hears the shot and watches the dummy fall with a splash into the lake and you could, at the same time, say *'leave*

Further Control

it' to the dog thinking that this diversion is simply that and the dog will not be required to pick it.

You then turn the dog, line it up and send it to the reeds to hunt for the unseen dummy. When the dog gets back, the judge says to you *'OK, now send the dog for the one in the water.'* You try, but your dog won't go anywhere near the dummy he and everyone else can clearly see floating in the lake. He searches everywhere else he can think of, to try and find something for you, whilst desperately trying to continue to obey your 'leave it' command, concerning the dummy floating before his eyes.

When the judge tells you to call your dog up, it's no good you then saying *'Well, I didn't know he was going to have to retrieve that one'!* Your dog may have made a spectacular retrieve on the blind but you would get 0 points as the double retrieve has to have both parts completed, otherwise it is scored as a failure.

If you need to give a *'leave it'* command, you should examine why this should be. If there is no reason, then stop giving the command. If there is a reason, then whatever the training issue is should be sorted out – now! When that has been sorted out, there should not be a reason to give the *'leave it'* any more.

In training and in exercises at Gundog Working Tests, distraction exercises may be any of the following, where a dog will be required to pick one item despite something happening to divert his attention: a distraction with a blind or a distraction with a mark and the most likely will be a distraction and a blind.

<u>Training and exercises.</u>

Having worked through exercises involving different combinations of doubles, most dogs are able to cope with distraction exercises relatively easily provided that strict adherence to obeying heel and sit commands has been applied by the handler. Any lingering problems in these areas should be addressed before moving on to these exercises. There may seem a point in moving on, as far as a handler is concerned, but it is much better to make haste slowly, always addressing any problems as they occur and making sure a dog fully understands each and every new phase before moving ahead.

At some time lingering problems *will* have to be tackled and unfortunately molehills will have turned into mountains; some of which will be impossible to reduce in stature once time has worked its magic and made them into concrete edifices!

When you start to incorporate distraction exercises into your training regime, there is no benefit in making the first distraction as wildly exciting as it is possible to get.

I have seen this happen in training classes and all that results is that either the dogs are so excited they run-in and forget all previous training, or handlers start resorting to shouting and blowing their whistles as hard as the whistle allows!

Maybe the dog gets the required dummy at some point during the mayhem, but I have always had difficulty in understanding or working out what the dog has actually learnt from the exercise. Usually, however, handlers have been delighted at the end result because *'well, the dog finally retrieved the right dummy!'*

Others will gather round and congratulate the handler saying things like *'yes, you had to work hard on that, well done'* and *'you did well to stop him getting the wrong one'* and most agree that *'well at least you won in the end and he got the right one'*.

For me the emphasis has always been concerned with *how* the dog gets a dummy, not the fact that he has got it! Surely training classes should be about teaching a dog what you want the dog to learn? Training classes should not, in my opinion, be about throwing dummies into as

Further Control

many different places as you can find or about dogs and handlers ending an exercise on what I would term a failure?

I could never understand the logic of these types of distraction exercises when I was first persuaded that was the way to do it, and I still can't! The reason given was that *'you have to make it like that otherwise it is not a very good distraction and you need to test the dogs'*.

I disagree. That to me, is setting dogs up to fail and then punishing dogs for actually achieving what I set them up to do! In other words, one sets out, knowing the dog will probably be so attracted by the distraction that it will go for it and in so doing, will be severely punished and therefore *learn* not to do it.

What a long-winded and totally unfair method of teaching a dog. It is training a dog by punishment and is an attempt to teach a dog what he is *not* to do i.e. go for the distraction. Yes, learning can and does take place by these methods, but for me it is a bit like hoping a child will get run over by a car, in order to learn he should not play on the road! A kind of *'there, that will teach you'* after an event which injures or hurts or *'let that be a lesson to you'* which was one of my mother's favourite expressions when I did something as a child and it all went wrong!

There are easier, kinder and, I think, quicker methods to ensure learning takes place with children and dogs!

I prefer to teach a dog what he *is* to do and that is obey me *no matter what is going on around him,* and I teach the dog this: by praising him for what he does correctly in terms of his obedience to my commands; but also by setting up the training environment for him so that as far as possible he learns the lesson I am trying to teach him. Uppermost in my mind has to be *'how is my dog going to learn the one thing I am trying to teach him on this exercise?'* The working out of how this is to be achieved will never be concerned with the dog getting the dummy! It will never, either, be concerned with *'how can I make sure my dog does this wrong so I can inflict a punishment!*

It will be concerned with the question *'will my dog obey me?'* If the dog obeys me, does what I want; then he will be praised, then he will possibly get another reward of being allowed to get the dummy for *me*. He will also learn; and the one tool used to enable him to learn, is praise for getting it right even though I have set everything up to almost guarantee he does get it right!

If a dog gets it wrong, I believe this is always my fault, never the fault of the dog. It is my fault for giving my dog an exercise to learn something before he was ready for this next step; not thinking out the exercise carefully; not thinking of another step on the pathway of learning which I should have incorporated; not finding precisely the correct place to set up the exercise; not stopping the dog or the exercise quickly enough *before* the dog got it wrong; not stepping in to act appropriately at the first sign of things going wrong; or not reading and knowing the dog sufficiently to ensure I set the exercise correctly for that particular dog.

I also believe, as an instructor, that if things go wrong it is usually my fault.

I have to think about how to set something up so that the dog can learn what he needs to be taught. More importantly, however, I have to set things up so that the handler can be taught and learn. If the handler is unable to learn, the handler will be unable to teach the dog correctly.

Praise is the 'wonder drug' of dog training whereas punishment, although having a place in certain situations, is such a severe form of treatment that the side-effects can create more problems than it solves.

Further Control

For handlers, *success* is often the wonder drug needed, and having even a small success enables handlers to persevere - even when the going gets tough!

However, back to what I now believe you should do. The hardest type of distraction exercise is a distraction and a blind. It is better not to start with this but start with a mark and distraction, which should almost be the same as a double mark in terms of the chain of events for the dog, the only difference being that the dog does not retrieve the distraction!

🐾 A mark and a distraction.

Start with your dog on a sit in the heel position. Face on a diagonal line approximately 10 to the hour and have a dummy thrown on that line, in front of you, at a fairly short distance. Then turn, with your dog at heel, still facing the front, but positioned on a diagonal line at 10 past the hour.

Have a dummy thrown on that line in front of you at a longer distance than the first dummy. Turn with the dog at heel back to face the first dummy, line your dog up and send him on a 'go back' to retrieve it.

Once the dummy has been correctly retrieved and presented, turn with the dog at heel, and give your dog a sit command. At this point, the dog will think he is going to be sent for the other dummy. Up to this point everything has been the same as practiced previously on a double mark but the difference now is that the dog will not be sent for the other dummy.

Remind your dog to sit, praise him, and then turn and watch, with the dog, whilst a dummy thrower picks up the distraction dummy. Praise your dog.

Everything in this exercise uses what the dog already knows. He may be slightly puzzled why he was not sent to retrieve the remaining dummy however, this too was an aspect of training to which he should have become accustomed, because you will have continued throwing dummies and picking them up yourself, on occasions.

Your dog will now have completed a mark with a distraction. Yes, there is more to it than this in terms of embellishments but he and you will have achieved this quietly, consistently, with no punishment necessary, no shouting, no blowing of whistles, and the dog will have begun to learn what you want him to be taught. He deserves a lot of praise for this.

Diversion dummy
X

Dummy to be retrieved
X

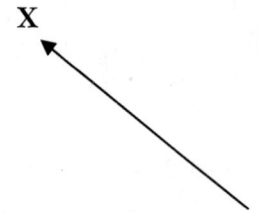

Dog/Handler

When practicing this exercise it is important for the handler to continue facing forward when the second dummy is thrown.

Learn to adjust your body position sufficiently to be on the correct line, but do not make the mistake of turning round in a complete circle first.

Moving your feet and body a few degrees left or right will ensure the dog puts himself in the correct heel position to see the dummy, but also ensures that the dog understands this philosophy without a

Further Control

handler creating a great deal of self inconvenience, by having to moving more than is necessary.

🐾 A blind with a distraction.

This exercise goes one step further than the mark and distraction, but only a small step. Every piece of the exercise uses aspects of training which the dog already knows and has understood. The only difference is that some of the pieces are used in a different order.

Start by deciding on the diagonal lines you will use and have a dummy placed, as a blind, at a fairly short distance at 10 to the hour. Then go to the area with the dog and face the diagonal line of 10 past the hour whilst a mark is thrown at a greater distance from you than the position of the blind.

Whilst still facing the front, turn with the dog at heel, line him up and send on a 'go back' command to retrieve the blind.

Once the dummy has been retrieved and presented properly, turn with the dog at heel in the direction of the distraction and watch whilst the dummy thrower picks up the distraction dummy. Your dog has now completed a blind with a distraction.

Diversion dummy
X

Blind to be retrieved
X

Dog/Handler

Both these exercises could be finished, instead, where the handler leaves the dog on a sit and then the handler goes and picks up the dummy.

Either way will reinforce the message to the dog that these exercises are different and that others will be responsible for the dummy which he knows is still out there. I know some dogs get worried about leaving things. It may be silly but I believe anything which relieves the anxiety of the dog when you are teaching something new, can only aid their learning.

Once these two exercises have been completed there is no point in thinking that your dog can now understand all the complexities of diversions. These two exercises are the basic, bare-bones upon which more can be built.

You have to build up the experience for the dog in different situations so that the dog can learn and develop additional skills. What must never change is the obedience to the known, never changing commands. You need to teach the dog that circumstances will continue to change but commands will never change. Commands taught will remain the same for ever as too, will the handler's insistence that the dog obeys these commands always, without question, *no matter what*............!

Training and experiences should continue on all aspects and there is no need to do distraction exercises every time you go out with your dog. There needs to be a gradual progression in terms of complexity however and the following suggestions can be used as a guide to the type of exercises which can be incorporated:

- Use of a shot sound. A shot sound can be used to herald the mark or blind or the distraction, and then both the mark or blind and the distraction.

Further Control

- <u>Increasing and decreasing distances.</u> Gradually decrease the distance between the dog and the distraction, leaving the mark or blind to be retrieved also at a fairly close distance to start with. As the distance between the dog and the distraction gets progressively closer, the distance between the dog and the mark or blind can become progressively further away.

- <u>Other directional commands.</u> As the dog becomes more experienced the handling, in terms of retrieving a blind, can start to incorporate other directional commands in addition to the original 'go back' command. For example have the blind placed so that the dog has to go back along a track, is stopped and then sent to the left or right in order to retrieve the dummy. Make sure when this is first tried that your dog remains in your sight otherwise he may find a way back to the diversion.

- <u>Water.</u> Incorporate marks and blinds with distractions to include water experience.

This can be used as an additional distraction by using the sound the distraction makes as a dummy lands in water; using water for a mark to land in before a distraction; handling a dog into water for a blind after a distraction; using water for the distraction and a mark or blind.

All these exercises have to be built up with care however and there is no point in making an exciting diversionary splash into water close by for a dog which is a 'water idiot' or expecting a dog which is still not confident in water to be handled into water for a blind.

You need also to consider how you will get the diversion out of the water and a dummy tied on a length of thin rope is ideal or just throw a stone into water as the diversion. Use both these with care however (See Chapter Twelve). Build up gradually but also consider the dog in question, making sure that in developing experience on one aspect will not set the dog back several weeks on other aspects of his training, experience and confidence.

- **Angles.** Begin to decrease the angle between the distraction and the mark or blind.

When decreasing angles in this way you must be aware of the wind direction and make sure you are not sending a dog for a blind where the dog has to pass too closely to the distraction or has to pass an area where the scent will be coming too strongly from the distraction. Every exercise, in every place and on every day, must be thought out carefully to continue ensuring you give the dog the very best opportunity to learn what you want him to learn. The dog will therefore succeed simply by obeying your commands. This is team work at its best.

The dog, whilst learning, will continue to want to please you because he is praised and because, after obeying you, he may also have the additional reward of being allowed to retrieve a dummy or bird.

- **Other dogs.** A useful additional exercise to begin once a dog is gaining confidence with distractions is to have two dogs and handlers in line. This type of exercise is frequently encountered at Gundog Working Tests.

In training it is a useful exercise in steadiness as well as obedience in enabling a dog to further his understanding of obeying your commands whilst another dog is engaged in something which your dog would like to do too, or instead of the dog who is working!

In practice this exercise is strictly neither a double, nor a distraction exercise but a hybrid. The way it is set up is often as follows: Two dogs and handlers in line with each dog on a sit in the heel position. One dummy may be thrown as a distraction for dog number one, which then has to be sent for a blind in a direction away from the distraction.

Further Control

Once dog number one has successfully retrieved the blind, dog number two will be sent for the dummy which was used as the distraction for the first dog. The two dogs will stay in line and should swap places.

The exercise will then start again with a dummy thrown as a distraction for dog number two which will be sent for the blind and when he has completed this, dog number one will be sent for the distraction dummy.

When dogs are in line on this type of exercise, this is the occasion where if a handler says *'leave it'* at any point, that some dogs will get confused and yet one hears it said on so many occasions at Tests.

Both dogs should simply sit, as commanded, when dummies are thrown as distractions in this way. It should not be necessary for a handler to do anything, because it is not necessary for the dog to do anything other than watch, listen and then obey whatever command is subsequently given.

When dog number one is being sent for a blind after the distraction dummy has been thrown, dog number two must wait, without a command of any kind, simply because he should continue to obey the first sit command given, until he is given another command.

This exercise is similar to those used in walk-up situations where between two to six dogs may be in line at a time, only one dog is working and the other one to five dogs must sit and wait.

This type of training exercise is particularly useful, when water is used, as it removes the problems of how to get dummies, used as distractions, out of the water.

🐾 Another hybrid type exercise seen often in Gundog working tests is that of a dummy being thrown or a shot being fired when a dog is on its way back to a handler after retrieving a dummy.

Initially the dog could be sent for a mark or a blind.

Then, when the dog has retrieved this first dummy successfully a dummy may be thrown to one side, or behind, the dog.

The dummy may be seen or heard by the dog, but it will be thrown whilst the dog is running back to the handler with the first dummy.

Alternatively a shot could be fired to the side or behind the dog, but again this will be done when the dog is almost back to the handler with the first dummy.

Whatever is used; a marked dummy or a shot, the dog after presenting the first dummy will then have to be sent for the other dummy thrown or towards the shot to find a blind.

This exercise is therefore both a memory type double and a distraction type double: the dog will have to remember where the second dummy was thrown; or remember the direction of the shot; and he could well be distracted by the dummy being thrown or the shot being fired. Also, the handler must mark the dummy or watch and listen for the direction of a shot. If the dog has not marked the dummy, then handlers must be sure of its location, otherwise the handler cannot send the dog on the correct line of either the marked dummy or towards where the shot was.

When training for this type of exercise handlers must be ready to stop the dog either going for the dummy or going towards the shot *before* the dog has presented the dummy he has already retrieved.

Further Control

Ideally one wants the returning dog to acknowledge the next dummy or shot but to do nothing but hesitate briefly, watch or turn to see where a shot comes from.

You must reinforce the responsibility of the dog to return to you when he has something in his mouth. Handlers therefore need to be ready with the stop whistle command and/or a recall command, if it becomes necessary whilst also watching where the second dummy has been thrown or the direction of the shot.

Bebe
(Photograph: Anthea Lawrence)

CHAPTER EIGHT

**Bebe, daughter Sian and 4 of Sian's sons
(Photograph: Nigel Haines)**

Obedience – or obedience?

There is an old English saying: *'A woman, a dog and a Walnut tree; the harder you beat 'em, the better they be'.*

In many gundog circles the 'o' word meaning obedience, has long been the 'o' word meaning obscene. It is never said out loud in polite gundog societies and in traditional gundog training the word itself has never been a serious part or played a significant role. The meaning of the word is taught, in a fashion, and provided one did not mention the 'o' word, the practical aspect was evident in terms of how dogs behaved due to their learning of some of the principles of obedience.

During my early days of learning how to teach a gundog I was actually told things such as, *'oh, obedience is a waste of time'*; *'there is no point teaching a gundog obedience because they don't need it'*. This puzzled me at the time because I was witnessing competent handlers issuing commands to their dogs and, for the most part, dogs carrying out the action required of them. What was the process involved then? To me, the dogs were

Further Control

obeying and they must have learnt how each command was to be obeyed, otherwise they could not have carried out the action required.

The dogs were not, I reasoned, born knowing what to do. Further more if the dogs did not obey the command, some kind of punishment was applied, depending on the severity of the disobedience. For some reason I could never fathom, the word *dis*obedience *was* used, and this was a word which one could use in whatever gundog society one found oneself!

I could never get a straight answer to my questions concerning obedience other than *'oh, you don't want to bother with all that, we don't need it'* and all this did was further my confusion between what I was told and what I was witnessing.

Some of this confusion began to clear when I realised that although handlers were being encouraged to teach their dogs what was required of them, the way this was done left a lot to be desired, in my opinion. The reason for this was, as I later reasoned, because obedience was learnt by the dog due to the negative actions of handlers rather than being taught to the dog by a handler teaching in a positive way and yes I witnessed a lot of what I now believe to be ill-treatment of dogs and met many of the beat 'em brigade!

People also spoke openly of dog-breaking. They still do! Perhaps not *how* it was or is done in explicit terms; but certainly in terms of wanting dogs to do things not required later, and then breaking the dog of the habit. The two things were seen as important and necessary: the first to improve speed, enthusiasm and hunting abilities; the second to gain respect through fear. The two aspects were seen as a pre-requisite for creating a better working gundog and necessary, in fact vital, otherwise a perfect gundog could not emerge as the end product.

Having spent my professional life working with parents and children, I was all too familiar with the type of learning children received in some homes, due to similar methods being utilized. This was mostly that no-one ever taught some children the correct way to behave; the children therefore did as they pleased until it became a nuisance to an adult at which time the child was shouted at or hit or arrested.

The children therefore learnt, sometimes, not to do some of those particular things again, certainly in view of that particular adult, because they were punished. Sadly, many continued doing those things, continued being punished and spent a lifetime being at odds with society in general. In simple terms: adults were trying to teach children not to do something, by punishing them for doing it rather than systematic, positive and consistent teaching and example about how they *should* behave.

A child, as with all living creatures, is equipped, from a very young age to learn, and all a child needs to learn things desirable from the perspective of a law-abiding and civilised society, is a responsible person to teach them, an environment geared to provide the correct experiences and positive role models. The converse is also true and children, who were not taught and did not have the correct environment to learn appropriately, still learnt but learnt all the wrong things in comparison with the things expected.

I have never seen a well-rounded, competent, law-abiding adult emerge from a child who was encouraged to do all the wrong things and then have the habit beaten out of them.

I then applied this philosophy to my thinking concerning gundogs and realised that many of the dogs and handlers I was observing were exactly the same as the so called 'problem' children and their parents with whom I had worked for the previous 20 years.

Once I *saw* what I was seeing it was glaringly obvious, and my perception was that most handlers were teaching the dogs using punishment. That is the dogs were learning how *not* to do something

Further Control

and how *not* to behave in order to find out *how* to behave, and, depending on the nature of the dog, they were using guess work to understand what a handler wanted.

Some dogs inevitably gave up even trying to find out what was required of them. For many dogs the sad fact was that they had to experiment a great deal before finding the correct or desired action or behaviour and unfortunately, every experiment, which resulted in the wrong action or behaviour, was punished. These were the dogs, which appeared to have been rewarded for exactly the same things, before the day came when *'today is the day that this dog is going to be broken of the habit.'*

Some dogs never managed, consistently, to find the correct behaviour and avoid the punishment, some suffered the inevitable final release from their troubled lives and others were moved from home to home.

All that happened when the dog managed to perform the correct or desired action was that he did not get punished and the only reward for a gundog was to be allowed to retrieve sometimes and they certainly were never praised for retrieving as it was felt that the retrieve was reward enough. For the dogs who had given up trying they were rejected as being unsuitable and many were re-homed or worse!

What I witnessed, on the whole, was some dogs which learnt, eventually, *not* to take a certain action because they were punished but if managing, by some fluke, to get the action right were given no indication that they were correct, other than not being punished.

Unfortunately, I continue to witness this in so many situations and it sadly is not a thing of the past. Wherever I go I see dogs being roughly handled, severely punished for doing very little wrong and treated on the whole as though they are some kind of enemy by the person they probably love the most.

I am not ashamed to say I love my dogs, even when they are being disobedient, wilful, doing things I wish they would not! They are my companions, they are my team mates, they give me a huge amount of pleasure and opportunities that I value and would not want to miss. They are not there to make me look good, or bad for that matter and I value them for what they are – dogs!

I also know however that loving them is not enough. Love carries responsibilities one of which is discipline but to me, if a reasonably sane, human of average intelligence cannot train and discipline a gundog without resorting to kicking and beating the dog, then that person really has no right to own a dog.

I am not denying that dogs, as well as ourselves, learn by making mistakes and learn too sometimes, by punishments. Morally I cannot justify punishing a dog before I have taught him in a positive manner and before I am sure he has learnt what I believe I have taught him, any more than I could condone parents and others using similar methods for children. Equally, I will never now, knowingly encourage an undesirable behaviour and would certainly never reward a particular behaviour with the express desire to *'knock it out of the dog later'*.

Even when I have taught a dog and I am sure he has learnt, I will not use physical punishment. I have done, oh yes, but not any more because I now know that often physical punishment can escalate. Dogs can get used to being punished. They become resigned to the fact that whatever they do they are punished. If they do not know how to avoid the punishment, and many won't because they have not been taught what *is* required, the dogs continue to do more of the un-required things. This in turn creates a handler who has to make the punishment more severe.

Handlers too can get used to punishment in terms of the fact that having used a physical punishment on a dog, if it appears not to have worked, the answer is seen as having not done it hard enough!

Further Control

This is the aspect that worries me more than any other when I think of electric collars and the opportunity presented, by these modern instruments of torture, for some owners to give more and more electric shocks to a dog and go on increasing the severity of this.

I have seen dogs which have been traumatised by the use of these collars by so-called professional trainers, and others. For some people they are seen as absolutely brilliant because they no longer have to go through the effort of kicking or grabbing hold of the dog.

These are dog-breaking kits advertised currently as 'remote trainers'. Quite an innocuous name until one realises what they are!

What they are not, are dog training instructors in touch by email with their pupil handlers, despite what the new, user-friendly name may suggest!

Earlier I mentioned that dog-breaking was the traditional way for gundog training and although severe dog-breaking may have ceased in part it has, unfortunately, left behind a legacy of using punishment as a teaching tool, so much so that people do not even realise that they are using punishment as a means of trying to teach a dog. Traditions are difficult for people to leave behind and because some things have worked they continue them, with no or little thought about what they are doing, why they are doing it or how they are doing it.

One only has to examine rules and regulations for competitive activities with dogs, as set out by the Kennel Club, to see an example of a legacy left of the dog-breaking and sometimes cruel methods employed by gundog trainers, to realise that there is recognition of this contained within rules governing gundog activities to this day.

In a Field Trial a handler is not allowed to carry a walking stick without permission from the senior judge prior to the Trial starting. In practice, this is given only after a fairly lengthy discussion involving, it sometimes appears, ones entire medical history. A competitor must be able to convince the judge that a walking stick is needed for medical reasons, and one cannot walk without it. Can you imagine any other sporting body, writing in its rules and expecting a competitor or participant to request permission to carry a walking stick?

Now, why should this be?

If one examines all the other rules and regulations for every other dog activity currently run under rules and regulations issued by the Kennel Club, one can find no reference at all to the fact that a handler may *not* carry a stick whilst engaged in Agility, Obedience, Working Trials, Heelwork to music, Fly-ball or any other activity be it a competitive or non-competitive event.

The reason is that everyone knows, but few will say, that historically gundogs have been trained using a stick to punish them. Historically?

There are numerous regulations and penalties in force to deal with anyone found to be using methods which are not deemed humane. These are contained in legislation as well as rules of the Kennel Club and it is certainly true that contained within all rules and regulations of the Kennel Club, for every dog activity, there is one rule which states that no physical punishment may be used whilst engaged in any competitive or non-competitive activity governed by the Kennel Club.

Why then, I wonder, is it still deemed necessary for mention to be made that handlers may not carry walking sticks in most working gundog activities?

The conclusion can only be that it is believed, by those in the Kennel Club who make or change the rules, that people continue using a stick to correct, discipline, punish and abuse gundogs. The rule therefore seeks to give those who do so, no unfair advantage in a Field Trial by using a stick as a permanent threat to a dog of its use, whilst under

Further Control

Field Trial conditions. The rule also seeks to punish those who need to use a walking stick, for legitimate reasons, in what are sometimes difficult conditions. It is only handlers wanting to compete in gundog activities however, who are penalised in this way.

Once a population stops doing something or behaving in a way deemed to be wrong, and the activity has largely disappeared for as many years as others can remember, laws usually disappear from statute books because there is no point in updated them. If there was the belief amongst the majority of gundog trainers, instructors and judges that such methods of training were truly buried long ago in history, then the legacy which lingers in present day rules, would surely have been removed many years ago along with many other rules in general, laws which no longer apply to modern day society.

Originally I presumed that when I was told not to bother with obedience, it was because people were thinking of Obedience, meaning competitive Obedience. Seeing dogs work in competitive Obedience gives many clues as to why this type of Obedience is not appropriate for gundogs; particularly in regard to the heel position and the need for a sit to be perfectly positioned as well as a retrieve exercise with a finish for the present which is far too close to the handler for comfort.

The need for obedience however in terms of a dog obeying commands instantly, is a totally necessary part of a gundog life and totally a part of life for a handler with any dog.

Maybe I was told not to bother with obedience too because the teaching methods beginning to emerge in the numerous dog activities available, were reward based and in many ways, were a long way away from the traditional methods employed in gundog circles.

Reward based teaching can appear, to some people, to take longer than using punishment when a dog does something wrong but another facet of training was beginning to emerge also and that was to begin training a puppy when he was young. This too was a facet of gundog training which was almost unheard of because many dogs were sent away from home to be trained at the age of 6 months or older by professional trainers. For those who trained a dog themselves rather than have the dog trained for them, many breeders continued the theory that the dog should not be trained until between 6 months and a year old. Consequently those acquiring a gundog puppy believed that *'because the breeder said so'*, they should not attempt to provide any training or guidance for their raw material for fear of ruining the dog for training later.

This theory concerning allowing the dog to please himself and certainly not doing anything which could be classed as *training*, continues to this day unfortunately. Many of the dogs we see in a training class are frequently those whose breeder advised their owner, *'you must not train him until he is a year old. You must let him be a puppy'*.

These dogs too are the ones with whom owners are experiencing severe problems and that fact is the one which frequently brings them along to training classes but at a time when instructors would prefer not to see them!

I use punishment. I believe that it is the reverse side of the coin labelled 'training' but it is the 'tails' side of the coin rather than the 'heads' and it is not my initial teaching method. It is part of the necessary learning process for the dog however and a way of communicating to the dog that what he is doing, or about to do, is incorrect or unacceptable behaviour.

My initial teaching tool is one of showing the dog what he must do and every single time I show the dog what to do, *I praise him*. Showing a dog what to do is essential, but what speeds the learning is the praise. Demonstration and praise are the only teaching tools necessary and those two are the ones which should continue to be used until certain that the dog has actually learnt the aspect being taught.

Further Control

Once I am sure of this then, and only then would a punishment be used if the dog did not comply with a command, because at that point the dog would be showing disobedience. At this point I need to make it clear that the punishment used, at most, is a growl! Sometimes this is a loud, fierce growl; sometimes it is a small, warning growl and with some dogs a look, as though I am going to growl is sufficient deterrent but there is never any kind of physical punishment. Physical punishment is abuse and as such there should be no place for it in dog training.

I know that some people will not know, or be aware, that some of the ways they have of teaching a dog are founded in using punishment as an initial teaching tool.

Many people, who feel they train in a humane way, simply mean that they do not use severe, physical punishment. That statement alone however does not tell the whole story and still says nothing about how they *do* train. I am therefore going to give some examples of this and show how with even very basic commands with a young dog, the dog is expected to learn initially by punishment.

- The method of teaching a dog heelwork by putting the lead on the dog and walking without saying anything.

Many people do not believe in speaking very much to a gundog and do not therefore give a command word. If no command is given, because many people do not believe in teaching any kind of 'heel' command, the dog has no way of learning where he should be. He has no way of learning when he should be in the position, other than by guess work, and no way of learning what the position is called.

Consequently he has to be on constant alert for when his handler decides to move so that he can try to get it right. If his handler then decides he wants to move without the dog he will also be punished very often because having started to understand that *'when the leader moves, I move'*, suddenly the leader will appear to change the rules but with little understanding of what the poor dog is to make of it all. The dog will be punished if he doesn't move when he is supposed to move, and punished if he moves when he is not supposed to move.

When no-one says anything to indicate what is to happen either time, the dog will have numerous punishments. He will also have no way of predicting what and when things will happen which may involve a punishment!

- The method of teaching a dog to sit by coming to an abrupt stop after walking and pulling the lead upwards and backwards until the dog has to take up a sit position.

Some dogs sit to avoid the severe pain inflicted on the neck and throat in a backwards direction but they are also then in danger from the upward pressure. Would you sit if someone had a noose round your neck?

Some handlers put a command word to this but usually only after or during the process of pulling the dog into this position. The command, if given, may in itself be a punishment: firstly in terms of its position in the chain of events, which is after the punishment by lead is applied. This is totally unjust because the dog is punished first, then given the command. Secondly in terms of the tone of voice used, which is usually in a harsh, loud voice.

Inflicting pain physically in terms of the pressure involved by using the lead in this way, and pain on the ears by using a deafening voice means the dog is being punished twice in an attempt to learn one thing.

Punishing a dog for doing what you want him to do, appears to have no justification and no logic either because a punishment is meant to deter not encourage. It is interesting to note that one of the dictionary definitions of punishment is 'severe handling'!

Further Control

Some handlers do not put a command word to the action for a sit. They use the same method for getting the dog to take up the position but do not use a command word. Their theory is that the dog must learn to stop and sit when the handler stops walking. This again has very little to do with dog training but a great deal to do with those who may wish to Trial and they believe in speaking as little as possible to the dog. Again the dog has to learn by punishment and has great difficulty in understanding where he should be or what the procedure is when he is *not* required to walk with his handler except that at these times he will often be shouted at and this will then be a 'sit' word or 'stay' word.

Neither of these words will have been previously taught to the dog but because he has done wrong, he is supposed, at this time, to know what the words mean. If the dog does not guess, after all the applied punishments, what position he should adopt, further punishment will be inflicted in terms of being hit with a lead or stick, being kicked or roughly man-handled in some way.

All the above are seen at almost every class or competitive event. Children use these methods, having copied their parents or because they handle a dog trained by a parent and the dog therefore knows no other way. The punishment, for some dogs, becomes the command and also, unfortunately, becomes just part of their life.

There are many other instances of behaviour such as the above but because heelwork and a sit are fundamental to almost every dog activity these are the behaviours of the dog which are often worked with first.

The first formal training many dogs receive is therefore immediately concerned with punishment and I feel that the word obedience, to some people, means punishment. The two words are synonymous, for some people, and because no-one admits to using physical punishment on a dog, they do not want to explore the meaning of obedience.

It is quite interesting to examine some of the numerous methods used in dog training today and examine what dogs are actually taught as well as how they are taught. The end product need not have any bearing on methods, so in theory a dog could be taught using any one or more different training methods leading to any one or more desired activity or competition.

The pet market has seen a tremendous upsurge of recruits for training in recent years and with this an upsurge too of methods which depend on a reward-based philosophy.

Unfortunately, in my opinion, much of the reward-based philosophy leaves a lot to be desired when it comes to assessing whether or not a dog is obedient to commands. The truth is that many are not obedient and the reason they are not, for the most part, is that the dogs are frequently not taught a command word, and/or they are not taught how to obey.

Many are taught by luring them into adopting a particular position with a tit-bit or toy, and this, once taught has to continue for life otherwise the dog won't do it! Because lures of this type i.e. food or toys are not able to be used in competitions, nor, I may add, in my classes, handlers have to pretend to the dog that the food or toy is hidden in their hand. The handler has then, to go into all kinds of strange manoeuvres with the hands, feet and body trying to coax the dog into a desired position. The handlers cannot therefore simply stand still and say 'heel' to the dog and then expect the dog to do it.

Trying to teach classes, where some handlers have learnt these methods, is quite a performance, particularly if trying to do a walk-up or similar exercise. One handler trying to get her dog back into a heel position, prior to the line moving on, can take up to 5 minutes of manoeuvres and still the dog is not sure where he should be in relation to the handler. Add this onto the time then taken for the same handler to get the dog to walk in the heel position, off lead, stopping and

Further Control

starting at irregular intervals and the whole scenario becomes quite a night-mare!

Those who teach clicker training would argue that their methods are entirely humane, reward-based and successful. Yet in many ways the dogs are punished far more, and much more frequently, than dogs taught using a different reward-based system but one which leaves the dog in no doubt what a command means, what the dog has to do to obey and when he has to obey.

With my reward-based training methods the dog is taught the command word, is shown what to do when he hears it and he gets the reward immediately – praise, my approval, my smile! These rewards I have with me always. They don't need to be bought, cooked or kept in a bum-bag; I do not have to remember to take them with me every time I go out and there is a never ending supply of them to be used whenever appropriate and wherever the dog is.

With clicker training, the dog is not shown what to do, he has to guess. He could guess six times and all the guesses are wrong and he will have to go on guessing for every new aspect of training thought desirable. Each guess he gets correct and he is rewarded, but the dog will have been punished many times for each one reward he is given.

The dog is not *given* a punishment as such so it is not positively punished but he is negatively punished by being denied the reward.

Withholding something, which is seen as a reward, is a punishment and as such one dog could, in effect, be punished 6 or more times for every one reward.

For me: obedience is everything and without it there is nothing.

I will reward a dog 600 times possibly in the process of teaching one action and I will continue to reward and reward until the dog learns.

Only then would I give one punishment if the dog disobeys me concerning something I am sure he has learnt and then the dog will continue to be rewarded for each and every correct response to one of my commands, every time, every occasion, everywhere he is, for the rest of his life, *no matter what!*

The beauty of praise as a reward too, is that it can be given freely to the dog and it doesn't make them put on weight! It can be given even when he is two fields away, in a wood, in the middle of a lake – in fact anywhere, *no matter what*............

Food and toys can only be given when a handler is next to the dog.

Many handlers willing to describe problems with their dog will mention many, many aspects of behaviour which they see as separate problems such as the dog will not: walk to heel, sit without being told 6 times, come back when he is told, bring a dummy back, hold a dummy without spitting it out, get into water, get out of water and numerous others.

Handlers see these as separate issues but I see them as only one.

If these problems are looked at in terms of commands they are that the dog does not obey: the heel command, the sit command, the recall command or the hold command. In simple words he does not obey the handler and why should he? Most dogs have never been taught to obey and then they are shouted at because they are disobedient. No wonder some of the dogs keep as far away from their handler as possible.

Despite what others may view as a whole range of different things a dog can do wrong; a dog can only do *one* thing wrong in my view and that is to *disobey me!* In my view therefore dogs need to understand the principles of *obedience* before they can ever understand the principles of *dis*obedience.

Further Control

I have, to my shame in the past, gone along with views and expectations of those whom I believed to know what they were doing. I have used punishments on my dogs in an attempt to teach them something but I hope never again to fall into this trap. I hope too that others may examine their own dealings with their dogs and be honest in their examination of what they see in themselves.

If you do not like what you see in yourself regarding whether you teach your dog using punishment as an initial teaching tool; if you are guilty of inflicting pain on your dog simply because you are getting cross; if you have not got the patience to teach your dog exactly what you want, in exactly the same way, for as long as it takes for the dog to learn, then perhaps you should change. Now!

If there are people, and I am sure there are many, who believe that pain and abuse is not necessary to teach a dog; who believe that dog-breaking in any shape or form should cease; then we should start speaking out, and against, those who still practice these methods. Have the courage to challenge those who you may see using punishment on a dog, but first have the courage to look at yourself with honesty.

The British legal system has legislation in force concerning penalties regarding beating women and dogs. There is no legislation, as far as I am aware, concerning the beating of Walnut trees!

**Bebe, daughter Sian and 4 of Sian's sons
(Photograph: Nigel Haines)**

124   Anthea Lawrence

Hand Signal positions

Hand positions such as these are frequently seen and used by handlers for the stop whistle and the 'watch me, because I am going to tell you what to do' command. Such hand signals may be visible to a dog when close to the handler in bright light; at further distances however, with the added problems of dark light, handlers wearing dark green against a green background, it becomes difficult for the dog to see.

Look at the same photographs from the dog's view-point and you will begin to see, and understand, the problems for the dog.

Further Control

It is important to change the body outline when giving a hand signal so that the dog begins to understand, and is therefore able to obey, when at greater distances from the handler and in dark light. These hand signals should be used always so that they never change, whatever the circumstances. This is the correct way for the hand signal, combined with the stop whistle/watch me command, to be given.

Look at the same photographs from the dog's view-point and you will see that this change in body outline makes life much easier for the dog as there is no doubt what the command means even if the dog cannot hear your voice.

On a 'go back' from the handler's side, it is important that the handler stretches the arm out fully. The hand should point in exactly the direction in which the dog should go and the handler should keep the arm and hand both rigid and still. The hand and arm should remain in position until after the dog has been given the verbal 'go back' command and has left the handler's side. Note here that the dog has left the handler's side but the handler, although having started to stand up straight, still has her hand and arm fully outstretched. This is the correct position for the handler and it ensures that the dog goes along the correct line.

Once the dog has retrieved the dummy or bird, the handler should stand in position and wait for the dog to bring the retrieved item back. Note the handler has her hand in position ready to receive the dummy. The dog should finish by 'presenting to hand' and releasing the item once the handler holds it and gives the 'give/dead' release command.

(Photographs: Anthea Lawrence)

Further Control

CHAPTER NINE

Jasper
(Photograph: Sarah Tunnicliffe)

Directional commands

During the basic stages of training, directional commands; some of which are verbal, some hand, some whistle and some a combination of several of these, are as follows:

- The 'go back' command which means *go away from me in a straight line.*
- The 'get on' command which means *go in a straight line, either left or right, depending on which arm I am using.*
- The two types of recall command which mean: (a) The quick recall *Return to me as quickly as you can* or (b) The slow recall *Come towards me, as I am going to give you another command and/or help you.*

Hand signals have been made using an outstretched hand and arm either directly above the head, as in using the stop whistle and on a 'go back' command, or at 90° to the body with the left or right arm as in 'get on' commands or in a line with the dog's nose and eyes when lining the dog up for a 'go back' from your side.

Hopefully, you are making sure that any hand signals you give to the dog, for the stop whistle and 'go back' commands at a distance, or from your side, are being given clearly and with the arm fully outstretched.

I need here to clear up a point made by someone to me only recently and that concerns a misunderstanding this person had of my description in *'Taking Control'* regarding a 'go back' from the handler's side.

I saw someone lining the dog up with the arm out-stretched but then with all the fingers held back by the thumb, and only the index finger visible. This particular handler believed that was what I meant when I said, *'the hand should point in the direction of the dummy, or where you want the dog to go'*. This hand, I believe, should be fully outstretched so that the *whole* hand points in that direction. This means that with the dog on the left, the dog then the dog looks along the line of the flat part of the palm of the handler's hand.

For hand-signals used when the dog is at a distance from the handler, changing the body outline is extremely important so that the dog can see and it is totally clear, from your body language, what you want the dog to do.

All of these commands have been to help the dog, as much as possible, to have a clear understanding of what you want and what is required. They have also been saying to the dog *'watch me because I am going to give you another command, and/or help you'*. The commands have begun to take on this meaning because you should not have given another command to the dog unless, and until, he does look at you.

Hopefully when your dog has looked at you in this way, you have smiled, and said 'good boy' as it is these factors which ensure the

Further Control

continuation of your dog looking at you. It is not too late to begin this process again, if by some chance you have forgotten to do it lately!

This is a reward to the dog for looking at you and it is a small enough price to pay to ensure that whatever you do, whenever you say something, whenever you blow your whistle, your dog looks at you eagerly saying *'yes, I'm ready, what do you want me to do?'*

So although you have not specifically taught the dog to watch you, he has learnt to do so. Once a good bond has developed between a dog and handler, you will find that your dog will be totally aware of where you are and what you are doing. You will seldom have to wait for your dog to look at you as you will almost *feel* him looking and willing you to say something to indicate that he may do something for you.

Having taught the dog basic 'go back' and 'get on' commands you will find that initially, these are adequate, combined with recall commands, to get your dog to correct areas. These commands are straight line 90° commands on a north, south, east or west basis.

Straight lines are necessary, but diagonals and different angles are important when the journeys leading to where a bird or dummy may be and the retrieves themselves, become more complex. Areas where you train, and where competitions are held, may also dictate the use of enhancements to these basic commands where a dog may have to go a specific route in order to get to the area a dummy or bird has fallen.

In theory it should be possible for a dog to leave the side of a handler on 360 different lines depending on the accuracy of the handler setting the dog up correctly. In practice this is not necessary but *diagonal* lines, for when the dog is being directed or re-directed when at a distance from the handler, are necessary and become more necessary as you begin to take *'Further Control'* and your dog is able to understand and complete several steps on a journey towards finding a bird or dummy for you

In combination with a straight 'go back', a straight 'get on' left or right, and a recall; diagonal lines back left, back right and forward left and forward right, start to become essential otherwise your dog will only ever be able to go in straight lines of 90°.

If you refer back to teaching a dog the 'go back' exercise, it was necessary to look at the position of a dummy from a handler point of view in relation to the dog. With the dog facing you at a distance, if the dummy was behind and slightly right of the dog you used your right hand to direct the dog. If the dummy was behind and slightly left of the dog, you used the left hand to direct the dog. These were cues to the dog in terms of the direction he should go. These commands were always used, however, with the hand held directly above your head.

In this, and other ways, the dog has learnt that your hands are an important aid to him in terms of the help you are able to give. Your hands must be obeyed as well as your voice and whistle. You will possibly have noticed that as your dog matures and begins to understand the significance of which hand you use that a remarkable change occurs.

If you set up a 'go back' exercise, in the beginning the dog will turn off the spot in indiscriminate ways to go back and retrieve the dummy. That does not matter because it is the turning round and going away from the handler which is the lesson being taught. As time goes on, you may notice; when you use the stop whistle and put your hand and arm up, that the dog will begin to turn slightly to the correct side, in response to seeing which arm you are using, almost as they get up from the sit position. The dog therefore turns immediately to the left or right from his starting position as soon as he sees your arm but of course he should not *get up* until you give him the verbal command in conjunction with the 'go back' hand signal.

Watch your dog and you may well see this developing. It is a wonderful sight as well as a total reassurance to you that the dog

Further Control

understands what your arm is saying to him. It is also a sign for you to be very careful and consistent about your arms and hands. This is why it is essential to monitor your own body language at all times to avoid inadvertent signals which could trigger an unwanted response in the dog.

Many handlers learn the hard way when it comes to inadvertent signals when they hurry to get a handkerchief out of a pocket or they talk to someone and wave an arm in the air. The dog takes these as a signal to go and if a dummy has been thrown or a bird has been shot, that is where he will go, not because he is a disobedient dog, but simply because he has learnt well. Unfortunately, sometimes the handler has not! This is a situation where punishment really *can* be an aid to learning! The handler, having been put out of a competition in this way, will never make that particular mistake again – hopefully!

The use of the correct arm in relation to the dummy and dog, should now be a totally consistent part of your handling and if not, you need to monitor yourself and ensure that this is so. If you have doubts about your consistency in this get someone else to watch you over a few training sessions and point out the times when you may be going wrong.

It is amazing how many people do not think first, before sending a dog away from them. One sees an alarming number of handlers who: use the wrong hand on numerous occasions; or have to fumble around getting themselves sorted out. Their dogs then get fed-up with waiting and go off and do their own thing! The handlers then wonder why their dog is going in the opposite direction to that required, doing everything wrong, being disobedient, *'deliberately to upset me!'*, they think. Of course it is always the dog which is seen, *by the handler,* to be at fault!

Handlers need to think, not only in terms of how an exercise should be done, as far as helping the dog, but also their own part in the proceedings. Fundamental to this, should be gathering their wits and equipment – before starting! Fumbling around with hands or trying to find a whistle, which is hidden underneath layers of clothing, is not acting in a professional manner as a dog handler!

For example: if a handler knows they have to send a dog back in a straight line from their side but then has to stop the dog in order to direct him along a track on the left, then: the handler must think first, should automatically stop the dog at the correct place and use the left hand and arm in conjunction with the stop whistle. This means that before sending the dog, the handler should hold their whistle ready and in the right hand so that the left hand is free to give the correct hand signal. This in turn means the correct arm is already indicating to the dog that his next move will be on or towards that particular side.

Of course the dog does not know, at the stage of stopping, whether he must turn and go back left, go directly out to his right (as he will be facing the handler at this stage) or even come forward right. He is already thinking however that whichever of the three commands he will be given: go back, get on, or slow recall that he should turn towards that direction. This is an excellent sign for a handler who knows that the dog has learnt this important aspect about hands and arms but it should also be a worry to handlers who have been a little inconsistent in these matters previously.

Some handlers use their right hand and arm in conjunction with the stop whistle in this situation. This means that as soon as the dog stops and looks at the handler the handler will be giving the wrong cue to the dog because the dog will immediately look at the handler's arm and start thinking his next move will be some command to his left. These dogs will therefore begin to look and turn slightly left on stopping.

Again, this should be an excellent sign, except for one crucial aspect and that is that the handling was wrong, and therefore the dog was being mislead at best and being set up to go wrong at worst!

Further Control

Some people may argue that whichever hand and arm is used does not matter, because at that point the dog should have stopped anyway, and this gives the handler the opportunity to change arms from the right to the left, and then send the dog in the correct direction to his right. This is true in part, but if a handler constantly misleads the dog he will begin to believe the handler is not competent and cannot help him. He may stop responding to the stop whistle, may stop but not look at the handler or may simply ignore whatever command is given next. In other words the trust starts to disappear. With a little thought and much consistency, a handler can be one or more steps in front of the opposition in competition, if their dog is already thinking along the correct lines.

For a dog to believe he has a competent pack leader he must be given evidence of this in all aspects of his life or he will begin to believe the pack leader job is becoming vacant! Like all good dogs he will need to fill the vacancy fairly swiftly because the pack needs a leader.

The other flaw in the argument comes when, for example, there are two dummies out.

Imagine you are told that the dog needs to stop in a certain place as above but instead of one dummy on a track to the left there is also a dummy on a track to the right, which is not required. If the dog is stopped at the correct place, but the handler uses the incorrect right arm in conjunction with the stop whistle, it means the dog will anticipate being sent to his left. If the wind is also coming from his left he may be picking up the scent of a dummy which will give further strength to his thinking that he will be sent somewhere to his left. There would at this stage be two cues being given to the dog and both would be incorrect, concerning what is required of him next.

The likelihood is that such a dog will simply wait for the 'get on' command without bothering to check which *way*, because he thinks he knows which way given the cue all ready given by the handler and the even more appealing motivation of the scent of the dummy.

This situation could occur on a shoot or in a Field Trial when there are two birds shot and one is dead and the other is wounded. In the above situation, the dog, given the wrong cues by the handler and the scent of a dead bird, would then retrieve the dead bird when it is the runner he should be pursuing.

When dogs get accustomed to looking at their handlers, watching hands as well as wanting to please, they start thinking and knowing what to do. Yes, they have to wait for the next command but it is all too easy for them to make a mistake when the 'get on' command is given and go in the direction they think they should go, because of the hand being used.

The dog will also add to this, information from his nose and if dogs have ceased looking at a handler too, all this will add up to a dog going in entirely the wrong direction. All this too, is totally unnecessary and requires remedial work when none should have been needed if the handler had been careful.

It is far better, in my opinion, for handlers to be totally consistent in their use of hands and arms in order to guard against such things but also to give the dog the opportunity to use his own skills to the advantage of the handler.

If a handler is totally consistent, it means that most dogs begin to turn their head slightly to the side in which they will be sent. One can see this turning of the head in most dogs in many situations because dogs point with their eyes.

They turn their head away from something to indicate they have no wish or intention of going in that direction or taking something which is in that direction. Conversely they look towards or at something to

Further Control

indicate that is where they will go or the direction in which something is located.

This turning of the head means that if the wind is in a favourable direction, the dog will also be picking up the cue from what his nose is telling him. He already thinks he will be sent in a certain direction, due to the hand and arm used by his handler and the scent will also guide him. When he is then given the 'get on' command, everything will point to him retrieving the correct dummy or bird and the whole exercise will look fluent and impressive, if it is for competition purposes, but above all it means wounded birds will be retrieved that much quicker.

Both cues will work for the partnership instead of a handler having to turn a dog away from the cues. In so doing, this will create handling problems which will be far more complicated than they should be and will result either; in whistle blowing, shouting or sometimes, the dog ignoring everything except what his nose is telling him, and that could mean getting the wrong dummy or bird.

Handlers also need to be aware however that should the wind be in a certain direction and a dog can wind a dummy at the place he is stopped, it can place a dog in a situation whereby he may disobey a handler's stop whistle and simply go and get the dummy he winds.

In training, this factor needs to be considered when setting up exercises. I will explain this in greater detail later and also show how this situation can be used to advantage with some dogs, or how it should be avoided with other dogs. (See Chapter Thirteen)

This may seem a long way away from the subject of diagonal lines but: if you cannot get your handling techniques correct, you are not up to the stage whereby you are 100% right, not occasionally but every time; your dog will not go in straight lines back, forward, left or right; then these are the aspects to work on first and then the embellishments can be applied. You cannot embellish something which does not exist!

Suppose you are trying to send the dog to an area where you know a dummy has been placed, or where you have seen a bird come down. You need not only to keep the end goal in sight, that is where the dummy or bird is; but also need to have a thought as to the best route.

You need to work out, sometimes quite quickly, the route the dog should take to ensure he gets to the fall, by the easiest, the best, or sometimes the only way possible, bearing in mind too the wind direction where the bird or dummy is lying. This is all to do with journeys and not retrieves!

It may not be the case that you can send your dog on a straight line from your side straight to the fall, due to there being perhaps: obstacles in the way, only one opening in high fencing, one track into a wood, one section of wall where the dog can get over, or one suitable entry point on the banks of a lake.

There may be other considerations too in terms of the lie of the land, so that if you send your dog one way he may be out of sight for a considerable time thus giving you no opportunity to ensure he continues to go in the direction you want. Sending him another way may be less direct but you can keep the dog in view, thus ensuring he continues to the fall in the way you know is best.

I mentioned in *'Taking Control'* about directional commands being concerned solely with a journey. They are a route which must be taken and this has nothing to do with retrieving.

If you were going on a journey; the destination may involve doing something, seeing something or getting something but unless you plan the journey with care you will never be able to do, see or obtain anything at the destination, because you will not get there!

Directional commands are the same. The dog cannot arrive at the destination (the fall) and be able to retrieve something unless the

Further Control

handler plans the route, is in control of the route and manages to get the dog, on his own, to the destination. Destinations cannot always be reached by going north, south, east or west because the roads or pathways or railway tracks may not exist in those precise directions. Sometimes one may have to go south-west to go south or north-east to go east or go north-west before going west.

Diagonals for dogs are the equivalent because sometimes the route directly east may be blocked by a wall or fence and taking a line north-east first will be required.

The majority of the time, the command you will be using most frequently is the 'go back' from your side.

Many handlers start to get a little casual about this command and start waving their arms in the vague direction they want the dog to go. The command, like all others taught, must remain the same *for life* and before starting any other directional commands, you should make sure that the 'go back' from your side is totally consistent.

Your own handling; giving clear, consistent, hand signals and verbal commands and the dog's responses to these commands must be perfect.

Usually if one of these factors is not perfect, then there will be a corresponding problem in the other. I have never found a dog which would deliberately go in the wrong direction every time he is sent.

I have found dogs which do go in the wrong direction and mostly this is due to a handler being inconsistent in the way the dog is sent out, moving their hand, or allowing the dog to go wrong initially and then trying to correct the problem by handling again at a distance.

Occasionally dogs do go in the wrong direction even though handlers do everything correctly. Dogs are not machines and they cannot be programmed to function in exactly the same way every time a button is pressed. They have their off days, they have days when they don't feel like it, they have days when they can't be bothered to do things in the way they know they should! They are dogs!

We humans are probably worse!

There are some things which we can do and there are some things which we know. We do not always do things properly and cannot always bring to mind things which we know, we know! We are not being disobedient concerning these things; we are not deliberately forgetting how to do something or forgetting information and facts on purpose.

Dogs are much the same!

If a dog goes wrong on something it is the handler's responsibility to stop the dog immediately something goes wrong; start again, and again and again. The handler starts again as many times as it takes for the dog to say *'OK, I suppose I had better do it you're way'*, or *'oh, yes, of course, now I understand what you want'*.

The handler must start again and do it exactly the same however otherwise the dog cannot grasp what is required.

This can sometimes be on something very minor but it is the very minor mistakes that should be the major focus for the handler to address. If the handler cannot be bothered to insist on the minor things, then the dog takes the non-intervention to mean, that the handler has changed the rule.

I shall give a few examples of these minor things in Chapter Fourteen, so that you may recognise in your dog and yourself, where you too may have to sharpen up a little. They are not huge problems and because of this, basics may start slipping, your foundations start to crumble!

Further Control

If you and/or your dog have problems in any of the areas mentioned, then you should work on these specific aspects to correct your own handling techniques, or make sure that your dog goes on the exact line you send him, before moving onto diagonals.

**Jasper
(Photograph: Sarah Tunnicliffe)**

CHAPTER TEN

Drift
(Photograph: Sonia Skinner)

Diagonal directional commands – Training and Exercises

Introducing a dog to diagonal, directional commands does not involve any additional commands to be learnt by the dog. What needs to be taught to the dog, and what the dog needs to learn; is that sometimes the commands he already knows will be given to him in new combinations, or there will be a different order and use of commands.

The dog will know all these commands separately but will need to gain experience of them being put together, as too will the handler!

The handler needs to begin to understand the relevance of different combinations of commands, as commands are the tools the handler needs, in order to help a dog on the journey towards the retrieve.

Further Control

```
          x
          ↑
  x  ←   Dog   →  x
          ↓
          x
```

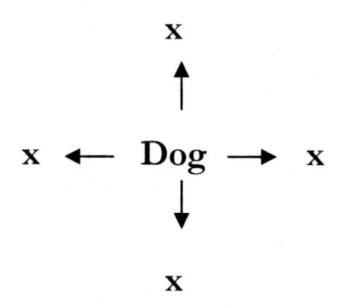

Handler

The above diagram is a representation of getting a dog to any of the dummies (x) in straight lines back, forward or sides. These should, at this stage be easy for the dog to retrieve using the commands of 'go back', 'get on', or a recall.

Training for the diagonal back command:

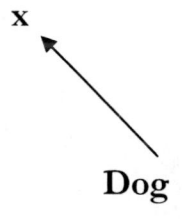

```
     x
      ↖
         ↖
           Dog
```

Handler

Position the dog on a sit, stand in front of the dog and have a dummy placed (x) in a diagonal line behind the dog to the left. Whoever is placing the dummy, should say 'mark' as the dummy is placed and it is better for the dummy not to be thrown. The reason for this is that you want to make sure that the dog obeys your command and is not simply going due to the motivation of the thrown dummy. After the dummy has been placed wait for a few seconds until your dummy placer moves out of the way.

This situation is not very different for the dog but what will be different is the position of the handler's arm. You should use your left hand and arm, first with a stop whistle with your arm outstretched above your head.

Then use a 'go back' command.

Drop your arm first, by bending it half-way so that your hand drops to the level of your head, and then immediately put it high up in the air to full stretch, but position your left arm at an angle rather than straight above your head. At the same time, you should give the verbal command of 'go back'. The hand and arm should be stretched to the full extent but angled at 10 to the hour.

Do not make the distance too far and make sure the dog can see the dummy. There is no point in trying to make complicated retrieves out of these exercises as that is not the training aspect needed.

Try to keep in mind what you want the dog to learn, and that is to continue to watch the direction of your arm and come to understand that this can tell them something more than they have already learnt. It is still a 'go back' command and must continue to mean *'go away from me'* but now the straight line is at an angle and in fact this command starts to take on the meaning also, of *'go away from the point where you are, in a straight line, in the direction of my arm'*

Most dogs manage to achieve this exercise with little trouble but if you have any problems, simply repeat the exercise once or twice in exactly the same way.

Next try the exercise by placing a dummy (x) in a diagonal line behind the dog to the right.

Further Control

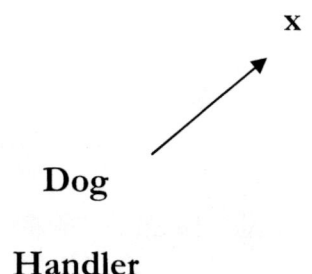

```
            x
           ↗
          /
    Dog  /

      Handler
```

This time you should use your right hand and arm for the stop whistle command. Then drop your arm to half-way as before and immediately put it up again but position your right arm at an angle rather than straight above your head, whilst you give the verbal 'go back' command. The hand and arm should be stretched to the full extent but angled at 10 past the hour.

These movements of the arm: from full stretch above the head on the stop whistle, dropping the arm to half-way, putting arm to the diagonal with the 'go back' command should be made as one free-flowing movement and not jerky, staccato movements.

You should also make sure that you leave your arm up in the air on the final diagonal until certain that the dog has moved off the spot, has turned and is going in the correct direction. Sometimes handlers drop their arm too quickly and if the dog notices this, some dogs stop because they think they have misinterpreted the meaning.

It won't matter, at this stage, if you leave your arm in position until the dog has picked up the dummy. It's much better to give the dog all the help you can, just in case he takes a quick look to reassure himself he is doing what you want. Later you may be able to put your arm down much sooner.

Having completed these two exercises, you cannot believe that your dog now understands what a diagonal line means, but you have begun to show him and practicing on diagonals will further his understanding of the help your arm direction will give him.

Once the dog is going immediately and accurately on the line you require, for a single dummy on either side, on a subsequent session you should place two dummies behind the dog on different sides.

It is advisable to have someone standing near the dummies in case the dog goes in the wrong direction. If the dog goes wrong someone should pick up the dummy before the dog gets to it. You can then pick up the remaining dummy, position the dog and then start again.

In addition to having people standing by ready to pick up dummies however, you should make it as easy as possible for the dog to pick the correct dummy because there is nothing to be gained from trying to complicate matters.

Have the first dummy to be retrieved placed nearer the dog than the second dummy.

Once the dog has successfully retrieved the first one, position him in the same spot again, return to your position and then send him for the second dummy.

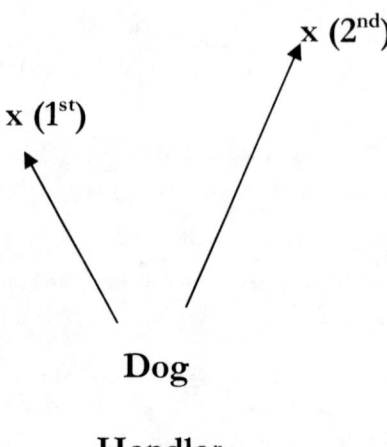

x (1st)   x (2nd)

Dog

Handler

Further Control

On a subsequent session you will be able, after the dog has retrieved the first dummy, to reposition the dog and put the first dummy back on the ground again before sending him for the second dummy. The first dummy can then be picked up by the handler or assistant afterwards.

These two diagonal directions are combined with 'go back' commands because the dog needs to go further away from the handler but goes back in a right or left diagonal line.

I have seen, and heard, handlers using a 'get on' command for similarly placed dummies. They move their arm from a ¼ to the hour, to 10 or 5 to the hour using the left arm; and from ¼ past the hour to 10 or 5 past the hour using the right arm. I prefer to use 'go back' as I believe this is more logical and I prefer to keep the 'get on' as a definite 90° movement for the dog.

Further sessions can include putting dummies at the same distance or put one closer to the dog, which you do not want, and one further away, which you do want. Training can then include blinds or dummies hidden in cover, combined with water, or anything which will further the experience of the dog and reinforce his learning concerning watching the direction of your arms in conjunction with going away from you on a diagonal line.

You should not try to make this complicated and should always keep in mind what you are trying to teach the dog.

If you can find two pathways in a suitable V – shape these are ideal as the pathways will help reinforce the direction you want the dog to take.

Do not place the dummies too far away because you do not want, or need, to get into a situation requiring more handling. If your dog does not go in the direction commanded on one command, and find the dummy, you have wasted the lesson. If that does happen however just stop everything and start again with the dummies closer. Don't get cross and don't blame the dog. Just simply start again and never be tempted to give an additional command.

The reason you should do this is that the exercise is not about getting the dummy. The exercise is to teach your dog about diagonal back commands and it is therefore about *how* the dog gets the dummy. Some handlers loose the plot sometimes and get into using different handling commands if it all goes wrong because they think the object is to get the dummy.

In addition to putting dummies in other types of terrain you should increase the distances. First of all you should increase the distance between yourself and the dog, leaving the dog close to the dummies. Then you should increase the distance between the dog and the dummies. Build up gradually and ensure success and if it goes wrong, shorten the distances again. What you must avoid is getting into a situation where you have to give an additional command to the dog on these teaching exercises. There will be other teaching exercises later where you can build in the use of several handling commands.

Training for the diagonal forward command:

The other diagonal directional commands concern coming towards the handler either on a left or a right diagonal line and these directions must be combined with a slow recall whistle together with a hand signal.

The other command which should be included on this particular exercise, is the 'hie lost' hunting command. This command is usually necessary for most dogs because some are reluctant to pick up a dummy on recall particularly if this has not been practised before. The dogs seem to think it is some kind of trick to catch them out and this is most common with dogs which have not been taught the difference between the two possible recall whistle commands.

Further Control

If you have only taught your dog the fast recall command to mean *'Return to me as quickly as you can'* then that is exactly what most dogs do, and good for them, because they are doing exactly what they have been trained to do. These dogs tend to ignore everything in their path back to their handler, and again this is a good point, because when a dog hears the quick recall command, that is exactly what he must do, get back directly and quickly ignoring everything en route.

It is not too late to introduce a slow whistle command to mean *'come towards me as I am going to give you another command and/or help you'*. With use, this command brings the dog forwards, but at a slower pace so that you can stop him more accurately, ready for the next command, than a dog which is hurtling towards you at 90 miles per hour!

This can be set up in the same way as practising a fast recall but using the new slow re-call whistle command instead and by aiming to stop your dog at a half-way point. Once the dog is responding to this you can introduce throwing a dummy to the side of the dog, or firing a shot. This acts as an extra incentive for the dog to stop as he then sees that something exciting happens when he does stop.

As well as the introduction to a slow, *'come towards me'* whistle, if you have not practiced getting the dog to pick up a dummy on a basic, straight slow recall then that is the place to start.

Set your dog up and leave him in a *'sit'* whilst you walk a distance away from him as though practicing a basic recall. At a mid-way point say *'mark'* and drop a dummy on the ground and then continue walking away until you are as far away from the dummy, as the dog is away from the dummy.

Don't make the distances huge. There is no point. Make the distance about 10 or 12 paces in total and you can then increase this once the dog understands.

Turn and face the dog and take a few seconds to consider what needs to be done:

The dog, when commanded, should come forward slowly on a slow recall whistle command, pick the dummy up on command and then continue his return to you; this time at a fast pace, on a fast recall whistle, to present the dummy.

The handler needs to give a reminder verbal sit command or a stop whistle and hand signal, followed by a slow recall whistle command. The handler should praise the dog for obeying the recall command, and then give the 'hie lost' command, or a 'hold' command when the dog is *six feet away from the dummy*. That means six feet away on his side, not when he has gone six feet past it! When the dog picks the dummy, he should be praised, and then if necessary given the quick recall command to return to you and present the dummy.

There are a lot of different things contained within this paragraph and you should make sure you know everything you are going to do, before you attempt it with the dog.

What the handler needs to be saying and doing is therefore: 'Sit, good boy'. Slow whistle re-call command, 'good boy', (for obeying the re-call) 'high lost,' 'good boy', (if the dog picks up the dummy, but not if he does not!) fast recall whistle command, 'good boy', 'sit, good boy', 'give/dead', 'good boy'.

Quite beyond many handlers it would appear when it comes to doing it! So, if you think you may make a mess of it go outside and practice on your own without the dog. The neighbours may think you have finally lost the plot but the dog would probably thank you for this little bit of effort on his behalf.

Further Control

All the above is important because you will only waste your own time and confuse the dog if you allow the dog to come straight back to you without picking up the dummy.

What you should not do, if the dog does go beyond the dummy, is try to stop the dog and then give him a 'go back' command, which is a fairly common mistake made by many people. The reason that you should not do this is that again, the exercise is not about getting the dummy, but about *how* the dog gets the dummy. Some handlers still revert to *'oh well, at least he got the dummy'!*

Think what it is you are trying to teach the dog, and stick to it!

If it goes wrong, you must stop everything. Think about it and start again making a few changes, probably in your own part in the proceedings!

If you are trying to teach a dog to retrieve a dummy when he is coming towards you, then that is the fact on which you should concentrate.

For those of you who have worked through the *'Taking Control'* exercises you will remember that when first introducing a stop whistle to your dog on a recall, I suggested that you be ready to walk towards the dog after you have given the recall whistle and before you give the stop whistle.

This exercise too is one where you should make the assumption that the dog may not understand he is to pick up the dummy, and therefore you should be walking slowly forward *after* the re-call whistle.

In this way you can give the 'hie lost' or 'hold' command whilst you are walking and you will be nearly at the dummy by the time the dog gets there and you can therefore encourage or at least prevent the dog running past the dummy to get to you.

If it all goes wrong and your dog goes past the dummy and returns to you, just praise him, although not excessively and take him back to where he was, take a deep breath, calm down and consider the situation.

Usually you will find there is something which you failed to do either in terms of the commands you gave or usually it is in the timing of those commands.

On this exercise, it is very rarely the fault of the dog. So consider how you can improve your performance and try again. It may help, if timing is the problem, to do it all without the dog! If you can find some other person to 'be the dog' for you it will help enormously. OK you may feel stupid, but it will help. This may seem a silly idea, but you do not want to practice it three times with the dog and get it wrong three times.

It is much better to get it wrong three or more times without the dog and not place the dog into the equation, until you are word perfect and have worked out when, and where, you will the give the correct commands.

If you consider your handling has been perfect and it was therefore the fault of the dog, this is easily remedied by the handler standing much closer to the dummy so that the dog picks it up on command when he is almost back to you. You can then start increasing the distance between yourself and the dummy on future occasions.

Once your dog can pick up a dummy on command, on a slow recall and you are both perfect then you can begin some exercises using diagonals on recall.

Position the dog on a sit, stand in front of the dog and have a dummy placed (x) to your left in a diagonal line in front of the dog. Whoever is placing the dummy, should say 'mark' as the dummy is placed and it is better for the dummy not to be thrown. The reason for this is that you

Further Control

want to make sure that the dog obeys your command and is not simply going straight for the dummy due to the motivation of the thrown dummy. After the dummy has been placed wait for a few seconds until your dummy placer moves out of the way.

Dog

↙

x

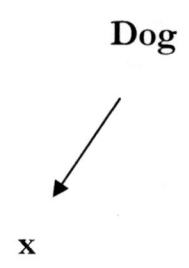

Handler

This situation is not very different for the dog but what will be different is the position of the handler's arm. You should use your left hand and arm, first with a stop whistle with your arm outstretched above your head. Then use a slow recall whistle command and immediately drop you hand and arm straight down, fully stretched, positioned at 20 to the hour. As soon as the dog starts moving forward you should praise him and, depending on the distance you will probably then have to say 'hie lost' or 'hold' as the dog will be 6 feet away from the dummy. This giving of the 'hie lost/hold' command six feet away is crucial because the dog will then be hunting for it in the right place. If the wind direction is coming towards the dog and scent coming to him from the dummy, this will also aid him in his task.

You can leave your left arm in position until the dog has picked up the dummy and if necessary you can then give a quick recall whistle so that the dog returns to you quickly for the present.

Once this exercise is completed, repeat the exercise but put a dummy on the right hand side instead. Remember to use your right-hand signal for the stop whistle first and then drop the arm at the same time as you give the slow recall whistle, positioning the arm at 20 past the hour.

On a subsequent session you can place two dummies, one on the left and one on the right. When you first try this make sure the dummy you want the dog to retrieve is nearer to him than the one you do not want him to retrieve and this way you and the dog will succeed.

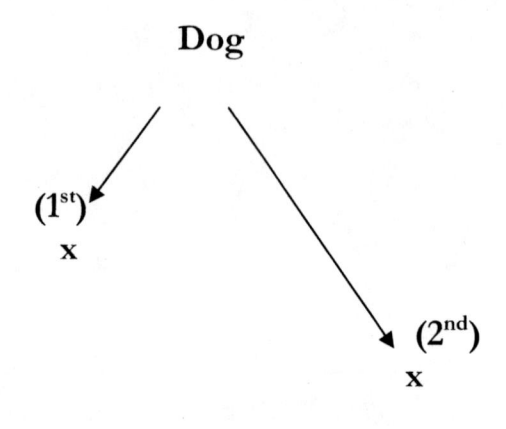

Dog

(1ˢᵗ)
x

(2ⁿᵈ)
x

Handler

Later, you can have dummies at the same distance or even put one closer to the dog, which you do not want, and one further away, which you do want. Further training can then include blinds or dummies hidden in cover, water, and any situation which will further the experience of your dog and reinforce his learning about understanding the importance of the position of your arms in relation to where you want him to go.

Some people feel that to practice retrieving on recall is an unnecessary aspect of training. They say that it is a training exercise which would have no parallel when the dog is working or in a competition. I feel they are wrong because what would happen if for example the dog is sent on a 'go back' command and the dog overshoots the place where a handler wants him to stop, or where a bird or dummy has fallen?

Overshooting the mark could either be due to the dog disobeying, or the handler not responding quickly enough in the circumstances. What would happen next however is that the dog then has to be stopped and

Further Control

brought forward either a small distance or many yards in order to be brought back onto the bird or dummy.

Sometimes this will then require a further stop whistle and redirection, but sometimes it is simply a case of getting the dog to retrieve on recall because he missed the bird when he was going back originally and this may have been because he was the wrong side of the wind. Bringing a dog forward left or right-handed can then take account of the wind thus bringing the dog back on the correct side so he will wind it immediately on recall.

It is worth mentioning at this point that bringing a dog forward on the correct side of the wind, may mean a handler giving a slightly different hand signal command. This again is a situation you must think out very rapidly.

There would be no point giving a dog a right-handed signal, with slow recall command if this would only bring the dog back on the same line he has already failed to wind the bird.

Taking account of the wind direction may mean you have to give a dog a left-handed signal together with the slow recall, even though you know the bird is on the dog's left as he faces you. This is simply because that is the direction he will wind the bird and will therefore turn to the correct side to retrieve it, once he winds it.

The hand signal will mean, as it should always, *'this is the direction you should take'*. It does not mean, necessarily, that, *'this is where the bird is'*. That is because all this directional work concerns the journey, the route which you require the dog to take.

It is the handler's job to figure all this out in terms of how best to handle the dog in order then, for the dog to use his superior scenting skills to locate the bird. The handler's job is to get the dog, by the best route possible, to the fall or to the area near the fall. This is where the dog will be able to work best to ensure, as far as possible, that he will locate and retrieve the bird or dummy for you.

Having a slow recall command, as apposed to having only one standard recall command, is much better in these situations I believe, for any dog, but especially if you have a very fast, responsive dog. Many dogs if they only have a fast recall do exactly that and handlers can get into a very messy situation of a yo-yo variety whereby the dog is recalled, sent back, recalled, sent back and the dog just keeps ending up roughly in the same positions every time.

As with all other aspects of training, I prefer to teach the dog all the separate factors about diagonals as different training exercises, give the dog experience of them and then if needed, out on a shoot or in competition I would not expect the dog to do anything he has not practiced and learnt to deal with.

As a separate, but linked, aspect of diagonal hand signals and commands; when you have taught your dog about retrieving on recall with a 'hie lost' command it is advisable to do some exercises whereby your dog does *not* retrieve on recall.

To train for this aspect you should set the dog up as for a basic recall exercise. Place a few dummies on the ground, near to you, so the dog will have to pass over them when he returns to you and practice a quick recall whistle. If necessary you may have to give your dog a 'leave it' command when he is approaching a dummy, but try the exercise a few times with the aim of teaching your dog that a quick recall is just that. He returns to you quickly and without doing anything else on the way!

After a few sessions of doing some straight, quick recalls with dummies lying around, when the dog should not touch any of them and some slow recalls with a 'hie lost' command when the dog should pick up the dummy, most dogs understand what is required of them.

Further Control   155

Putting these two exercises together after the dog has learnt each separately, seems to make the understanding for the dog much easier and they work out the difference for themselves and realise (a) on the slow recall there is a 'hie lost' given and he can retrieve (b) the fast recall whistle is different and because there is no 'hie lost' he can't retrieve.

When you get to the stage of trying the above two exercises it is very interesting to observe the point where your dog suddenly grasps the concepts totally. I have always found that the dogs also love doing these exercises and seem to enjoy the challenge of the situation. It is a very useful exercise to practice when several handlers and dogs are out training together too. Have a line of dogs and handlers with the handlers leaving the dogs sitting together at a distance.

Each handler should drop a dummy half-way between where their dog has been left and the final position of where the handler will stand. Handlers then recall their dogs one at a time, with the other dogs remaining in a sit. The first handler in line should give a slow recall followed by a 'Hie Lost' so that the dog picks up the dummy. After the present, this dog should be returned to the line and left in a sit with the other dogs.

The second handler will then give a fast recall whistle to their dog so that the dog has to return to the handler over the dummies without retrieving one. This dog should then be returned to the line to sit with the other dogs. Alternate down the line, for however many dogs and handlers there are, then do the whole exercise again reversing the order so that each dog completes both types of recall.

This type of exercise keeps handlers on their toes! They have to concentrate all the time and it also seems fun for the dogs. The dogs appear to enjoy the challenge, but it also keeps the dogs concentrating. They have to listen carefully concerning their own task, which is different from the task they have seen the previous dog complete. It is also useful practice for the dog distinguishing which whistle and verbal commands they should obey – those from their own handler; and which commands they should ignore – those from other handlers.

Drift
(Photograph: Sonia Skinner)

Further Control

CHAPTER ELEVEN

Bebe
(Photograph: David Tomlinson)

Water work

By the time you are at the stage of wanting or needing to do more advanced water work with your dog he will obviously be swimming well and will be confident in and around water. I say obviously, because unless he is swimming well and able to complete basic retrieves from in and over water then training should concentrate on these things first.

Some dogs seem to be much quicker gaining confidence in and around water than others. They all do it in their own way, at their own pace and if you have a fairly reluctant swimmer or one which has difficulty in entering water, then there is no point in attempting more than constant exposure to as many different types of water and locations as possible, doing the same things in as many different places as you can find. Water, as with other aspects of training, cannot be hurried. As a handler you must go at the pace of the dog on many issues and until a dog has learned what you are trying to teach, you must have patience and simply keep on teaching in the same way for as long as necessary.

Whatever the swimming capabilities of your dog, constant exposure to different types of water is a necessary part of their education and experience, and this should not be left too late. Dogs need to experience running water, water which splashes over rocks as it flows, water which makes strange noises and as many different depths and widths as you can find. I am not suggesting you should take young dogs to more testing conditions, or take those which still need to gain confidence in still water and small ponds. Dogs which have this confidence however, need to experience all types of water otherwise they believe that what you have shown them is all there is to water. The longer you leave experience of other water, the more likely your dog will have difficulties with it, and some may be frightened when water suddenly starts to take them away on a current for example.

Alongside different types of water, experience should also include experience of different vegetation found near water so that reeds, overhanging trees and plants become normal as well as sand, pebbles and rocks. The more you can show the dog, the better, so take every opportunity to expose the dog to: different kinds of banks into water; stepping over stones to reach the water; walking over rocks both to get into and out of water; and anything which may be part of the water scene such as boats, bridges, fishermen with bags, rods and lines – anything and everything!

Another matter to consider also is the style of a dog's swimming. No, I know we are not looking to give marks out of ten for this, but the style can affect the achievements of the dog and some young dogs, whilst being keen and having no fear of water, are extremely messy swimmers!

Some people believe that some breeds are more prone to swimming style problems than others but I have seen a variety of Spaniels,

Further Control

numerous of the HPR breeds and examples in Labrador, Golden and Flat Coated Retrievers. I think it is just a peculiarity of some individual dogs and it appears to me that it has nothing to do with breed, age or confidence although some dogs with bodies longer in length than the length of their legs, often appear to have a few more problems whilst they are growing.

I need to define what I mean by 'messy' and the main characteristic is splashing. This can range from a small amount because the front paws are only just beneath the surface of the water to something reminiscent of a paddle steamer going down the Mississippi!

Some dogs do not appear to be able to maintain the same body position in water, as they do on land. Consequently they almost lie on the surface of the water with the front half of their body, whilst allowing the back end of their body to drop downwards. It sometimes looks as though a dog may be walking on the bottom of a pond on his hind legs whilst his body is supported by the water thus allowing his front legs to be waved up and down first in the air and then onto the water surface and below. It looks exactly like a toddler sitting in a bath of water, splashing the water everywhere with his hands!

Unfortunately this style of swimming requires a lot of energy, and much is wasted in almost standing still. It should also require goggles and a snorkel!

Most dogs which may be messy swimmers in the beginning, actually improve with time and age and with some dogs, advanced water work may not be an option until this improvement is seen, particularly with the problems which involve a huge amount of splashing. I have seen handlers getting pretty irate with these dogs because they frequently do not respond to a stop whistle command or take any directional commands.

This is not because the dog is disobedient! The simple truth is that the dog is splashing so much he can neither hear nor see very much other than water and as there is very little one can do to improve the swimming style, it is better, in my view, to let the dog gain more experience and find out for himself, how to swim in a more efficient way.

The only thing that I have found improves this aspect with some dogs is to give the dog a heavier dummy or a larger dummy to retrieve. The weight tends to bring the dog into a better body position in the water and is a way of the dog teaching himself better techniques. It is best to experiment with this a little and judge for yourself the position of the dog swimming out, and then swimming back with a normal dummy first. Simply observe for a while to see whether there is a difference. If the dog is lower in the water, splashing less when he returns with a dummy than when he swims out for one, then it may be worth using a heavier dummy.

Simply changing what the dog is required to retrieve can be effective because they have to concentrate harder to bring in a heavier or different shaped object and in so doing, adopt a more natural swimming style which is not only more efficient, but shows the dog that he can get further, quicker.

Most dogs who are messy swimmers do not have other problems such as reluctance to enter water or any disobedience issues, so it is well worthwhile having some patience and waiting or experimenting a bit with different dummies. You should be careful though not to give a young dog something to retrieve which is too large or heavy in an attempt to improve swimming style.

Sometimes waiting for a dog to grow up is all that is required; so patience, exposure to different areas of water and allowing the dog to mature, are the things which will usually work whilst ensuring that you

Further Control

do not make a dog wary of swimming and retrieving simply due to your own impatience.

The aspects to consider and assess before going further and developing more advanced work, are as follows.

The dog should:

- Be totally steady when near water. No running-in, no noise or anticipating.
- Enter water confidently, in as many places as possible, whether by jumping in or walking and should not run up and down the banks excessively before making his entry.
- Retrieve a mark from in the water.
- Retrieve a mark which lands on the bank, the other side of water.
- Hunt a bank, reeds and other cover in and around water efficiently.
- Pick a simple blind from the water.
- Return to the handler quickly when either: he has picked up a dummy or in response to a recall whistle when he has not picked up a dummy.
- Return to the handler after leaving water, without shaking water from his coat other than for occasional problems such as water in his ears.
- Present a bird or dummy correctly without dropping it and as efficiently as after a land retrieve

There is no point in trying to do advanced water work with your dog if he has not mastered the above aspects and certainly no point in attempting any further advances with water if you have not taken control on land.

Handlers should also carefully, and accurately, assess their own standards regarding water work. Advanced training is not only to do with the dog; it has a great deal to do with handling! You should, at this stage, be exactly the same concerning; your manner, body language, commands, hand signals, confidence and leadership in relation to anything concerning water, as you are in relation to anything concerning the land. If not, you will send alarm signals out to your dog and the chances are your dog will not be as confident or as obedient in or near water as he is on land. This probably has nothing to do with the dog and certainly will not be a dog problem!

Water work is no different from any other work which you are teaching the dog apart from the obvious fact, that it is more difficult to enforce commands, when your dog is in the middle of a lake. Those proficient in synchronized or cross-channel swimming, or who have no objection to getting their kit off in the middle of January and diving in to explain things, perhaps need not worry too much! If you are not a keen water baby yourself however you must have total control of the dog first on land! Then you need to have total control of yourself near water and ensure you are exactly the same as when your dog is working on land.

The dog needs to be able to follow all the commands learnt in relation to working on land, on water too. Water is simply another type of situation of which he needs to gain experience, in the same way as he learns about working in long grass, boggy land, dense cover and root crops. There are some dogs which associate commands with certain situations and most dogs have to be taught that commands apply in the same way in, beside and on water as they do in every other situation.

Dogs do not know this automatically, they need to be taught.

For dogs which have been swimming well from a relatively early age hopefully, you have been giving your dog most retrieves from the other side of water, and he should now be used to crossing over water on one command of 'get over' and be able to hunt the far bank on the 'hie lost' command.

Further Control

If you have given your dog too many retrieves *in* water, you may need to give him some more experience of getting *over* water to ensure that he will cross over and not just swim in circles whilst he searches. It is important to give this experience and extra training before moving onto other aspects.

If you have only been giving retrieves *in* water up to this point and then you go on to doing some advanced work which is again *in* water, it may be that later, it will be a difficult task to get your dog to cross over onto the other bank. So make sure you can get your dog to cross from one side to the other of pools, streams and lakes and can also direct your dog further back and/or to the sides once he has crossed over the water.

For the next stages we shall return to doing some work *in* the water and develop directional skills and use of the stop whistle.

Before any directional commands can be taught to, and learned by the dog, it is necessary for the dog to be able to be stopped, by the use of the stop whistle, on water. This may seem pretty obvious, but it is amazing how many people think, that on water the stop whistle has no place and they try to give directions without blowing a whistle first.

There is little wonder therefore that dogs pay not the slightest attention to commands issued, in louder and louder voices usually, by distressed and cross handlers.

For one thing, the dog is swimming away from the handler so cannot see the handler; secondly the dog usually cannot hear verbal commands due to the noise of the water and the noise he is making in the water. Put your head into water at some time, splash your arms around, and see how much you can hear!

It is important to remember that the commands you have been teaching the dog since the beginning, *are for life!* To the dog, it should not matter whether he is in a field, in a wood, in a field of root crops, in a lake, or in the middle of anywhere else. The stop whistle always means the same '*stop, look at me, because I am going to tell you what to do and/or help you*'.

We must expect a dog to respond in this fashion wherever he is but we must also have respect for the difficulties this poses for the dog when he is in deep water. He plainly cannot sit, and due to the nature of water there will be some circumstances where the dog may not be able to remain in even a semi-stationary position for very long.

We must also have regard to the age of the dog and his experience of water.

The minimum requirements when a stop whistle is blown, is that the dog looks at the handler and remains looking for a sufficient amount of time to take in the command which the handler gives, after the dog has looked towards the handler. What the dog does not need is a dithering handler not quite sure what to do next; neither can he hang around waiting!

In all circumstances the dog, as soon as he hears the stop whistle, will have to turn round in the water. Dogs never do backstroke or sidestroke so they are usually moving away from the bank, with their back to the handler, and therefore cannot see anything behind them; which is normally where the handler would be.

After the whistle is blown and as the dog turns, he will be looking towards the sound of the whistle. There is no point in a handler prolonging the waiting for the dog at this stage, so the handler should be indicating, by hand signal, almost immediately i.e. when the dog is turning round, where the dog is to go.

The waiting time may need to be lengthened slightly later, but not necessarily, other than for dogs which are perhaps a little over-anxious

Further Control

or anticipating your next command without ensuring they have made the correct assumption in terms of your wishes.

This situation is another where a handler must use the correct hand and arm, in conjunction with the stop whistle, as a cue to the dog concerning the direction he will be required to take next. The dog does not want or need to spend ages treading water in the middle of a lake or fast flowing river whilst a bewildered handler gets the correct arm into position or swaps arms around after giving the dog false information! If required to wait too long, most dogs will not wait. They can't wait and will therefore be forced into disobedience!

So, to be fair to your dog you should ensure that you have been doing everything correctly and consistently, come what may, in all circumstances, in every situation, without fail, wherever you are, whoever you are with, *on land first*.

Handlers can create water difficulties for themselves but particularly for their dogs by not appreciating the problems for the dog when he is in such an environment. Many handlers, unless asked specifically to think about the special problems with which the dog has to contend, do not understand how difficult it is for a dog to have to tread water for a long time whilst trying to keep their balance, trying to breathe, trying to see, trying to hear, trying to avoid drowning, wanting desperately to get on with whatever job is required and get back onto dry land again.

I feel we humans would have even greater problems should the roles be reversed! Maybe I should try this at a training session when waiting for a handler to sort their arms out or when they have forgotten their whistle! Now there's a good idea!

Sound too can be distorted over water and it is known that voice sounds can be very different when associated with numerous water conditions. A whistle sound tends to be less likely to change over water and due to the fact that the dog will only know two or three different whistle commands, there is less likelihood of the dog mistaking the meaning of any of them.

Once the dog has looked, even briefly at the handler, he will be able to link any verbal command given with an appropriate hand signal as confirmation should there be any distortion of sound creating difficulties for him. This is one reason why it is important for dogs to gain experience of obeying verbal and/or hand-signals on occasions – a belt and braces situation for occasions where conditions may make either hearing or sight more difficult.

This is nothing to do with water training, but a memory which suddenly comes to mind of an example of a dog being able to work on verbal or hand signals on occasions.

Bebe and I were in the closing stages of a Field Trial and having had a fairly exciting, final, drive for the remaining 5 dogs left in the Trial it was becoming quite dark and suddenly fog appeared almost from nowhere. The judges were muttering in a huddle discussing thoughts about not being able to finish the Trial. We competitors and dogs were shivering in temperatures which had suddenly plummeted to zero, muttering to ourselves things such as *'I wish they'd hurry up, so we can finish the Trial and go home'*.

Eventually the judges returned, by which time it was even foggier and even darker and even colder. We had all seen where most of the birds had landed, which was an area in front, but to the right of us, inside the release pen. The only access was across the field straight ahead of us, down a narrow track for a short distance and then through a low gateway on the right into the pen.

If the dogs went directly right they would be confronted by netting of 12 foot high, behind which there were about a dozen shot birds. We could just see the narrow access track straight ahead, could not see the

Further Control

gateway into the pen further up the track, and could not see beyond the 12 foot netting.

I and my dog were the first to be called forward and I remember thinking this was a bit of luck because as I saw it, conditions could only get worse. How wrong I was!

I had to think very quickly as I was walking up to the judges and knew I needed to send my dog straight ahead, even though she was likely to want to go diagonally to the right. I knew also that I needed to make an accurate guess about stopping her just beyond the beginning of the access track.

The access track was only a few feet long, with the pen gate-way on the right and dense woodland on the left. I only had one chance because I could see nothing beyond or to the sides of the access track. Stop her too soon or too late and try to push her to my right, and I knew she would get nowhere because of the netting.

She had to get to the track and then go up the track. She then had to go through the gate but she did not know there *was* a gate.

If that worked, I would then have to push her to my right with a 'get-on' command. The problem then, was that she would not be able to see me and my 'get-on' command could have meant left or right, because she would not be able to see my arm direction. If she went left I knew that was our chance gone for ever.

It's amazing how much the brain can process in a few seconds, whilst walking from the line, about 6 paces, up to the judges!

I sent Bebe straight ahead on a simple 'go back' command, slightly left as I did not want her to divert off to the right, where she knew the birds were! I decided first of all to stop her before she got to where I thought the access track was. That gave me a last chance to give her some indication of where she was heading for, by using my right arm, before we lost sight of each other. I then gave her a diagonal back with my right arm.

She turned, went back and I then had to guess when to stop her again. I blew my stop whistle: I could not see her, had no idea of whether she had stopped, but then gave her a verbal 'get-on' command. I just had to trust in her good sense at that point. She knew where the birds were, she would know I had done my best in terms of setting her off on the correct route for her journey. I then waited.

Then I waited some more.

There was no sound from ahead or coming from the direction of the pen. I had no idea whether my dog was still sitting where I had last stopped her; whether she had gone back too far; whether she had gone left; or whether she had gone where I had hoped, to the right and into the pen.

I then waited some more. I then waited some more.

One of the judges *kindly* came over and said, *'If you are thinking of doing something, perhaps now would be a good time to do it'*.

Not having a clue as to what the 'something' could be, and the judge didn't suggest anything either, I waited some more, thinking I would be told to call my dog up. There was then a muffled cheer from the competitors and spectators behind me and out from the gloom came my dog holding a wriggling, wounded, cock pheasant.

Yes, all right I admit there were a few tears on my face but you can't really help it in those circumstances - the cold air causes it you know!

I said earlier, that fortunately I had been called into line first and how wrong I was.

Further Control

The next dog to be sent had to be called up by the judges because despite being sent by his handler in the same direction I had sent Bebe, it did not go straight ahead but went off to the right where it tried valiantly to jump the 12 foot wire netting.

Whilst this dog was in the process of eliminating itself however, the fog mysteriously disappeared as quickly as it had arrived. It was still gloomy, but visibility was such that the access track and the opening to the pen were both able to be seen clearly. The remaining 3 handlers whose dogs, after being sent straight ahead, found their own way through the gateway and into the pen, arriving back with a bird each, with no handling after the initial command.

1st, 2nd and 3rd places therefore went to these three handlers and Be and I were awarded a Certificate of Merit. The consolation was, that even the judges apologised after the awards saying I had the most difficult task.

Most of the competitors actually believed we would have been given 1st place but there is no such thing as an easy or difficult retrieve in gundog work but only how that retrieve is accomplished. The first three places went to dogs which accomplished their retrieves unaided by their handlers, made it look easy and it was disappointing for me but, as everyone says *'that's Trialling!'*

This had been a situation however where without my dog taking a verbal command, with no other help, because she could not see my hand signal, there would have been no hope of my getting her to the area of the fall of the birds.

Now, back to water!

When training for more advanced work it is better to choose a day when conditions in the water are conducive to learning which means the temperature is reasonable, the surface of the water is reasonably calm and there are no difficult currents with which to contend. These things will have to be coped with later, but it is better to concentrate on the training issues you want the dog to learn rather than concentrate on experience of different conditions at this stage.

If you are trying to teach your dog something new, you need to make everything as easy as possible for the dog to learn that specific training issue and cut out as many other factors, which may hinder this process, as possible.

If not, and particularly with regard to water, many dogs will simply not do it. They know there is absolutely nothing you can do to make them, and you would simply be setting up a situation which not only encourages disobedience but, more importantly perhaps, will not enable you to teach the dog the aspects you want him to learn.

Bebe
(Photograph: David Tomlinson)

Further Control

Water experience

Experience of water needs to be continued to include different types and locations, different banks and means of entry.

(Photographs: Anthea Lawrence)

Playing together on occasions can help dogs to learn about: jumping in, treading water, currents, and turning round in water; all of which will help them when they begin more advanced training. *AND* it's good fun!

(Photographs: Anthea Lawrence)

Further Control

One should never forget that basic and advanced water training is simply a means to this end - the whole purpose of gundog training!

A trained gundog should be able to find, and retrieve birds from difficult locations. Here, wounded ducks are successfully retrieved from the waters of the River Wye in January.

(Photographs: David Tomlinson)

CHAPTER TWELVE

Tiggy
(Photograph: Mary Ward)

Water – Training and Exercises

Before you begin teaching a dog the meaning of a stop whistle in water it is a good idea just to check that your dog will enter the water on trust, simply because that is what you have commanded him to do. I believe it is preferable to test this on a simple blind without the excitement of the splash or a gunshot sound, because otherwise you cannot be sure the dog is actually going on your command alone.

With some dogs, although they are steady and wait for the command to go, it is the splash or gunshot which is their incentive, rather than simply obeying the command of the handler. The splash or shot was a necessary motivating sound initially in order to teach the dog what a 'get over' meant and to help less confident swimmers but now, you need to see whether the 'get over' has been learnt by the dog without additional cues, other than the water itself.

Further Control

Without your dog seeing or hearing, preferably without the dog there at all, throw a dummy into the middle of water as a blind. Bring the dog to the water and, standing a few yards away from the edge of the water, line your dog up to face the dummy.

When he is looking on the right line, give him a 'get over' command.

Once your dog has left your side, he should enter the water as soon as he reaches it and swim out for the dummy. You should not give any other commands other than perhaps a 'hie lost' command if needed. I say *if needed* because it should be part of your own training and discipline now, to drop superfluous commands. Sometimes handlers get into the habit of continuing some commands when they are totally unnecessary such as a 'hie lost' when it is obvious the dog is about to pick up the dummy, or a recall whistle when the dog has got the dummy and is coming back on a straight line, as fast as his legs can carry him.

These commands *were* necessary when you first started training your dog, as a way of teaching him what he should do. These commands should now only be used in certain circumstances or only when necessary. They are saved for when a situation warrants them.

That doesn't mean that you should not, now and again, practice and make sure the dog continues to obey them but they should not now be part of *'this is what I say when my dog is so close to a dummy he trips over it'* or *'this is what I do every time my dog has a dummy in his mouth'*,

Those types of superfluous commands can almost become part of the background noise for a dog and many dogs may cease to take notice of them. Consequently, when you really need them, the dog does not obey. So, if you do not need to use a command, don't use it! Save commands until you need them but then, use them!

If this exercise is successful, it will tell you that the dog understands the 'get over' command, understands picking a 'blind' from water and also knows that he should return to you directly, once he has something in his mouth. You will also know that the dog trusts you and is obedient to a single command, even though nothing else, other than the circumstances of being by water, has added confirmation to his understanding of what he should do. You now know that an incentive such as a splash or gunshot is not one of the motivating factors necessary before the dog will obey and you know that your dog will go on command, on trust, on obedience, because you have told him that is what he must do.

Now you can use this knowledge to begin a stop whistle command.

In a similar way to teaching a dog what the stop whistle means on land, I believe one should give the dog every opportunity to actually learn what you want him to learn, and that is to stop what he is doing, look at you, wait for the next command and obey that subsequent command. Yes, he knows this on land, (and if he does not, then this should not be attempted in water), so he therefore knows *what* to do and *how* to do it on land. Now he needs to learn what and how to do this when he is in water. It is necessary therefore to ensure, as far as possible, that you create an environment and set up an exercise, which will almost guarantee that what you want to teach the dog will be the thing he learns.

When I was taught how to teach a dog about the stop whistle in water, a dummy was thrown into the water with a great deal of noise, splashing and excitement, and the dog was sent on his 'name' command, as for a marked retrieve.

I was then told to blow my stop whistle before the dog got to the dummy, stop him and make him come back to me with a recall whistle.

Further Control

I and many others failed to stop our dogs and as a result the dog retrieved the marked dummy. I was then told, *'well, you'd better work on that; otherwise you'll have problems'!*

Yes, too right! I had just created them when, with a little thought, this may not have happened. Also, by being sent away and told to *'work on it'*, I had made the problem worse. I worked on it religiously every day with the same result and had actually reinforced the wrong behaviour so rigidly it was impossible, later, to eradicate it. Practice making permanent and not perfect in this case!

Unfortunately I did not give this much constructive thought until years later because I believed the fault was with me or with my dog or probably both of us!

I was told to continue making the thrown dummy as exciting as possible otherwise the dog would not learn. Questioning this in order to understand, I was told *'well, you have to make it exciting because if you blow your whistle and there is nothing exciting, of course the dog will stop because there is nothing to make him disobey. He's got to stop when there is something exciting otherwise he could chase game on a shoot'.*

As I understood it, the theory was 'tempt your dog as much as possible and make him disobey in order to teach him he shouldn't disobey.' This was again about teaching by punishment.

I have remained puzzled for many years about this philosophy. I could see no logic in this way of teaching; it is to me, completely illogical as a teaching and learning tool and even more ridiculous than doing it on land because unfortunately I am not one of those blessed with the power to walk on water! Even if I had been, it would have been unlikely that I could get to the dog quicker than the dog got to the dummy and, unlike on land, most dummy throwers were reluctant to throw a dummy from a position *in* the water and they were therefore never in a position to pick up a dummy.

As I saw it, when later I began to work out how the exercise could be made easier for the dog to learn, the method was creating problems not only in teaching the dog a stop whistle, but also in terms of being dishonest with the dog. The dishonesty comes in two ways: first in that I can see no reason why, if anyone wants a dog to be totally obedient, and surely that is what most people want, they should try at any time to teach a dog to be *dis*obedient? Test a dog, a person or anything to breaking point and it or they will break! This is actually called the theory of stress!

When a good bond develops between dog and handler the dog knows what his handler wants, often before the handler says or does anything. If a dog is able to do this surely we humans should also be able to do it! A handler must be able to read their dog and know what the dog is going to do *before* he does something. It is important therefore for handlers to think good and clear thoughts as well as putting these in verbal ways. If you *think* your dog is going to do something, he usually does. This works positively as well as negatively!

Imagine the confusion for a dog when he 'hears' the thoughts and then hears the verbal commands and other cues, when a handler is tempting a dog to be unsteady or to disobey a command? It will puzzle him but, if you have already taught him to be obedient, he will have to be obedient by disobedience. He will obey what he thinks you want, which is disobedience, simply because you tempt him to do it and are setting him up for this.

The second dishonesty is in that having taught the dog to retrieve a marked dummy on a name command, I believe it to be totally dishonest to change that; it is wrong to send the dog on a name command when you know *before* you send him away from you, that you will be trying to make him stop before he picks up the dummy. I cannot see how this could possibly apply in a shooting situation.

Further Control

On land, the argument for using this method was that if the dog did not stop, then the dummy thrower would pick up the dummy before the dog got to it. The dog did not get the reward of the dummy to retrieve and would therefore learn he should have stopped and if he had stopped, would then have got his reward! Quite a lot of thought processes for the dog! No wonder most were confused.

The theory is fine in only one respect which is that of the dog not getting the dummy to retrieve if he disobeys the stop whistle. In other ways this theory had many flaws: dummy throwers did not always get to the dummy before the dogs; some dogs started developing problems later in going for marked retrieves and lost the speed, became hesitant on marks, having lost trust in their handlers. Some dogs also became worried about dummy throwers, who often shouted at the dog, or ran towards the dog in a threatening manner and some even threw dummies at dogs which would not stop.

Above all however, dogs were unable to learn simply, gently and in whatever time it took to learn, about what they should do when they heard the stop whistle. Some dogs did learn, eventually, but only by going wrong and being punished. These were often the dogs who didn't really care who shouted and bawled at them and were often the dogs who would get the dummy anyway as they could outwit the humans determined to prevent it!

The way of teaching the exercise was therefore designed specifically to goad the dogs into going wrong and teach the dogs using punishment, as an initial teaching tool. Many dogs did go wrong. Many dogs continued to go wrong.

Unfortunately the same method was used on water too and because most dummy throwers do not like standing in the middle of a lake, for some reason, there was not the remotest chance of picking up the dummy before the dog got to it, should he disobey the stop whistle.

In an attempt to help with this problem some instructors then threw a dummy, attached to a long rope, into the water. The idea being, that if the dog did not stop, then the dummy was rapidly hauled in to the side using the rope. This too had more than a few problems in that frequently the dog already had hold of the dummy and was therefore hauled in too!

The other problem was that hauling the dummy in, even if the dog had not managed to get hold of it, created a moving dummy slicing rapidly through the water, frequently making a splash as it went! *Joy of joys'* thought the dog, *'a duck which I'm just going to have to chase and catch'*.

I remember laughing, along with other members of groups at the wonderful sight of a dog dashing through water in hot pursuit of this wounded quarry. I was inexperienced, naïve and had not, at that time begun to think *'what on earth, are we trying to do with these dogs?'*

On one occasion I remember a dog getting hold of the rope as well as the dummy and the dummy thrower was unable to haul the dummy in!

He valiantly kept hold of the rope and the dog was trying, very energetically, to pull the dummy in the opposite direction. Numerous suggestions were made as to the resolution of the problem whilst the tug-of-war ensued. Not all the suggestions are printable but most would either put the dummy thrower or the dog at risk! My money was actually on the dog at this stage as he seemed to have more enthusiasm for the task than the dummy thrower who was fast losing his grip on the situation in more ways than one!

Eventually someone came up with the bright idea of *'throw another dummy into the water'*. That suggestion was eagerly ceased upon like manna from Heaven, was acted upon and, much to the delight of most people, the dog dropped the roped dummy, which had suddenly lost its appeal, and went after the newly thrown dummy. A cheer went up from the waiting crowd and most people were delighted at the outcome

Further Control

when the dog finally retrieved the latter dummy and the dummy thrower retrieved the dummy on a rope.

I think we all went home at that stage! The mood was cheerful with everyone agreeing about how wonderful the training session had been.

Did anyone stop to think? The object of the training session and the specific exercise set up was *'how to stop your dog on water'*. As far as I could see the *'how'* was never really addressed because no-one did! No dog stopped! No-one was told or shown the *'how'* at any stage. All the information given was concerning the end product, if you like, i.e. *'the dog should stop when the stop whistle is blown'*. The exercise then became a test to see if the dogs would stop. It was not an exercise to teach the dogs *how* to stop at all.

It was all too easy to forget what we were supposed to be teaching the dog and all too easy to teach the dog everything we do not want him to do. In the process of trying to teach a dog one reasonably simple concept of turning round in the water and looking at his handler when he hears the stop whistle, these dogs were taught:

- The teaching regarding marked retrieves now has to be forgotten because sometimes it will mean something else.
- You don't have to do anything when you hear the stop whistle except what you were doing, OR you can even do something else which appears more exciting.
- You can retrieve anything you like.
- You can chase things which move in the water.
- You can swap dummies and game if something more exciting lands, OR you get a bit bored with what you already have in your mouth.
- You don't have to obey when you are in water.

It is a very impressive list and amazing to think what can be achieved in one teaching session! Unfortunately the one thing we set out to teach the dogs was not achieved. Never mind, there will always be another training session when we can probably reinforce all the above aspects and still not teach the dog that he must stop when he hears the whistle! Unfortunately, similar methods continue to be taught in gundog training sessions and clubs the length and breadth of the country to this day.

I do not teach the stop whistle in that way now, either on land or in water!

So, back to the way I do teach!

- Having successfully retrieved a blind from the water, line the dog up again to face the water and, with no dummy in the water, give him a 'get over' command. Once the dog is in the water and swimming, blow your stop whistle. Remember to do this only once but also remember to blow it with good volume to take account of the distance and the noise made by both the water itself and the dog swimming.

The dog will probably turn in a circle to look at you (he obviously can't sit). As soon as he looks at you praise him with a *'good boy'* in a loud voice, blow the stop whistle again as a reminder and then immediately recall him with a rapid recall whistle. All this should be done fairly quickly, but appropriately, and do not try to make the dog wait. The praise for the dog when he returns must be excessive but if all goes well it is important to give a *'shake'* command and the subsequent *'sit'* command too, before praising again.

Try to keep everything the dog already knows as part of the exercise, as that will give him confidence and boost his ability to understand the new part which has been added.

Further Control

The above is, ideally, what will happen; but dogs being dogs and handlers being handlers, the ideal is not always what *does* happen. So, what if your dog does not do it as above? The following may help:

<u>If the dog does not obey the stop whistle.</u>

Without blowing the whistle again just watch for a second or two. If the dog hesitated or made a slight turn he may be trying to do something in response to the whistle but is unsure about either what he is to do or, more likely, he will be unsure about how he *can* do it.

Any indication from the dog in this way and I feel it is best to put a *'good boy'* in as this will confirm to the dog that his thought of responding to the whistle was correct. The praise may be sufficient for the dog to continue turning and you can then complete the exercise.

Some dogs will only give the handler a split-second, in terms of their hesitation, when the handler should respond with praise. You need to read your own dog in this respect. I frequently have to read dogs belonging to others, and usually can tell a handler the appropriate time to respond, due to the fact that I see the dog trying to obey or think about doing something other than what he *is* doing. Sometimes I have praised the dog if I have read the signs and the handler has been too slow, and this has been sufficient for the dog to continue turning, allowing the handler to take over. It is more important however, for each handler to recognise these signs in their own dog and develop responses appropriate to the signs they are seeing.

If there is no indication from the dog that he has heard or is thinking of obeying by turning; and this will mean that the dog is continuing to swim with speed away from the handler and there has been nothing, even a faint glimmer of hesitation when the whistle was blown. A loud growl would then be appropriate, followed by blowing the stop whistle again. Subsequent hesitation or turn or look must immediately be responded to with a lot of over the top praise before the recall whistle.

It may be necessary for this sequence of growl and whistle to be repeated several times before the dog obeys.

You must not give up trying and must therefore continue for as long as necessary but, when the dog does respond, everything else should apply in terms of the praise for obeying and then the recall followed by more praise.

You need to forget, once the dog shows signs of obeying, all the disobedience before hand otherwise you will not be able to reinforce the final obedience sufficiently and appropriately. It is the praise which will teach the dog what is required and the praise which will allow the dog to forget what was *not* required, in favour of what *was* required.

Handlers can ruin this learning by continuing to be cross, due to the difficulties before the final obedience; so whatever the difficulties have been, paint the smile on your face and act delighted, when the dog does obey! Whenever he does obey, however long it takes, that praise must be given whole-heartedly!

You should then go back to some of the exercises concerning use of the stop whistle on land so that your dog understands that the stop whistle must be obeyed, wherever he is, whatever he is doing, *no matter what*.......

Then you must give the dog the opportunity to put that learning into practice by trying again on the water and measure whether improvements have been made. This series of practice on land, then water, may have to be repeated more than once

<u>If the dog does not obey the recall whistle.</u>

Some dogs are uncertain in these circumstances when they believe they have been sent into the water to retrieve something so, although they

Further Control

stop and look at the handler they then continue in their quest for a dummy. You may have to be fairly insistent about the recall and I would apply the same sequence as above so blow the recall whistle and if the dog disobeys, growl and then blow the recall again, following the same sequence several times if necessary.

You must not give up until the dog returns to you and it is important to insist, however long this may take. It is also vitally important for the praise to be given unstintingly, when the dog does return. It is the final part of this exercise where many handlers frequently go wrong in not giving the dog the excessive praise when he finally returns to them.

The handler is cross because of having to put in so much effort, so that, if they praise at all, it is a quick 'good boy' in a grudging voice. If you have a dog which needed a lot of encouragement to obey the recall, you need to praise excessively first and not be too insistent on the sit or shake commands.

What many people do not understand is that when a dog has disobeyed and it has been a struggle for the handler to win; when the dog finally obeys, however long this has taken, the handler must give six times the amount of praise, than would have been needed for a dog which obeyed instantly.

The human feeling is one of giving more praise to the dog which obeys instantly and no praise to the dog which has taken a long time, or has needed lots of commands and growls, before he complies with the handler's wishes i.e. the ones which put the handler through a great deal of trouble, pressure, hassle and embarrassment!

This is the wrong way round!

The philosophy may work with a child where explanations are possible and where one may want the lack of reward to a child to act as an incentive for next time but, *it does not work that way with a dog.*

You cannot explain to a dog; you have no way of saying *'if you come back quicker next time, then I'll give you your reward'*. There is only *now* for the dog, and if the now referred to, is the moment of arriving back to the handler, then that is the time he needs his reward and you must make it a big one.

The big reward will help to ensure that next time he comes back more quickly.

The equivalent of, *'you can't have a reward, because you were a bad boy'* will guarantee that your dog takes even longer next time.

The look of thunder on a handler's face, because they are still cross with the dog, will also guarantee that the dog takes longer next time. Would you go to someone who looked fierce and didn't talk to you in a pleasant way?

If your dog comes back, and arrives to see you looking very, very cross his view of the situation will be *'my handler is cross with me because I have come back'*. Add this onto a dog which believes he should have brought back a dummy from the water then you have a recipe for disaster!

So paint on the smile, it is important! Above all, remember the BIG reward. If I were in that situation I would be down on the ground kneeling down to welcome the dog back with as much praise as I could for a good few minutes. Have a play, get wet, but make your dog feel he has just done the best thing he has ever done in his life and you have appreciated the fact and are proud of him, and think he's the best dog who ever lived!

If you have had any problems you should go back to working on recalls on land with your dog in as many different places as you can find

Further Control

so that your dog understands that the recall whistle must be obeyed, wherever he is, whatever he is doing, *no matter what*.......

Hopefully, if you have made sure that your dog has learnt about obedience and you have ensured that he obeys all your commands instantly, on land, you will not have any problems and if problems do occur then you will have insisted, and won in the end. You should also have ensured that you recall the dog sometimes, even though he has not retrieved a dummy. Otherwise you will have taught the dog, inadvertently, that from his point of view, *'I only obey the recall whistle when I've found the dummy or bird'* and *'If I haven't found a dummy or bird, I don't go back, no matter what my handler does or says'*. Any difficulties at all must be addressed on land again first before returning to the water.

Training should, after this first exercise has been completed satisfactorily, be continued as follows:

- Line your dog up to face the water (there should be no dummy out at this point) and follow all the steps up to blowing the stop whistle. This time after you have blown the stop whistle and the dog looks at you, praise him and throw a stone into the water as far out to the left or right of the dog as you can. It is even better if you can get someone else to do this for you but their timing has to be good and the stone thrown immediately the dog looks at the handler. Your dog will immediately look towards the splash, so then you should blow your stop whistle again, get the dog's attention and praise him and then recall the dog with lots of praise for obeying.

- If your dog comes straight back to you on command. You will know that the dog understands the 'get over' command, will obey the stop whistle and recall and this time you know he understands more of the *no matter what*.... Because there was great temptation put before him in terms of investigating the splash.

If your dog makes any attempt to go towards where the stone landed you will need to growl, shout 'no' or use your 'leave it' command and make sure he understands he is doing wrong. There will not be anything for him to retrieve but you need to persevere with recalls and growls, until your dog returns to you; when he should be praised – excessively! Some remedial work may be necessary, depending on the severity of the problem:

1. Go back to basics exercises of steadiness: with the dog at a distance throw balls, dummies, toys all round the dog and recall him over the objects; heelwork with objects being thrown; leave dog with a quick sit, roll a ball and recall the dog whilst the ball is still rolling.
2. Sit your dog on the bank of a pond and throw a stone over his head to make a splash in the water and then recall the dog.

Whatever the problem is, it would be advisable not to continue water work until you are sure the dog will obey you before you try again from the point before the problem was encountered.

Then you must give the dog the opportunity to put that learning into practice by trying again on the water and measure whether improvements have been made. This series of practice may have to be repeated more than once

Progress should then be continued as follows for all dogs, once the steadiness aspects and correct responses to your commands are working well. It may take a while to get to this stage and it is well worth waiting if there are even slight problems because when things get more exciting, disobedience can escalate rapidly.

Further Control

- Sit your dog on the bank of the pond (as in 2 above), stand in front of him and throw a dummy over his head, into the water. Recall the dog and when he is back to you line him up for a straight 'get over' to fetch the dummy.

- After the dog has successfully retrieved the dummy, send him in the direction he has just been, with 'go back' and 'get over' commands. There is no dummy now, so when he is approaching the area where the dummy was, blow your stop whistle.

Immediately the dog responds, by hesitating and/or turning round, praise him and give him a 'get on' command out to the left or right, whichever is the most appropriate or convenient, depending on the space and access concerning the area you are using.

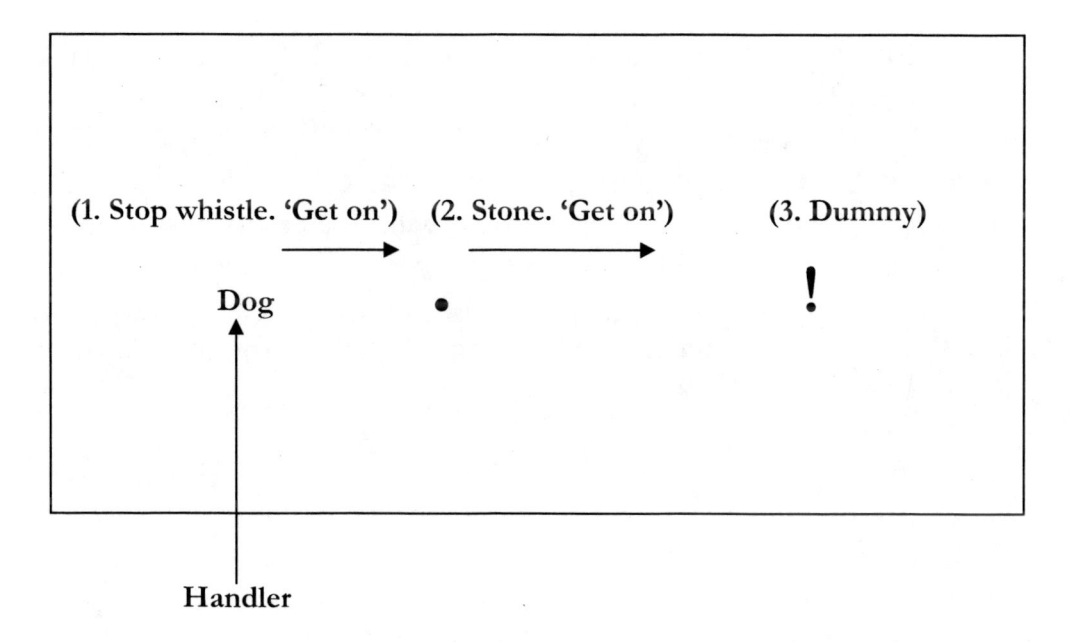

(1. Stop whistle. 'Get on') (2. Stone. 'Get on') (3. Dummy)

Dog

Handler

Once the dog turns and starts swimming in the direction you have indicated, you should then throw, or have thrown, a stone out to the side to which he is swimming, a few feet in front of him. You should then repeat the 'get on' command, and praise. The stone should act as a motivating factor and accelerate the dog swimming. A second or so later, you should then throw a dummy out to the side, another few feet in front of the dog, repeat the 'get on' command with praise, and let the dog retrieve the dummy. This is a way of showing the dog what you want him to do. He starts to obey the command first, gets the motivating splash of the stone, continues to obey you, then gets the motivating splash of the dummy which he gets then as another reward. The exercise should then be completed in the normal way as far as the return and present.

As a result of your first session or sessions you will have certain information:

1. You know that your dog is steady to something thrown into the water when *he* is in the water.
2. You know the dog understands the principle of obeying your last command even though he has not completed the command before that.

For the next session try and get a friend to come with you. Tie a length of cord to a dummy. This dummy will be a diversion not to be retrieved and the cord will enable the dummy to be pulled out of the water afterwards! Yes, I know I have had problems with doing this in the past, but there are benefits in using this, provided the other aspects have been taught first!

Throw an ordinary dummy to the right in the water then throw the diversionary dummy on the rope, to the left. Make sure that these are well apart and the angle between them is as wide as you can get although the diversion on the rope, should only just be in the water on the edge. If it has to be pulled out by the dummy thrower this should not take a long time and it should not become an exciting, splashing, half-submerged, water-monster toy which goes yards and yards through the water. You should make it so that apart from the initial small splash, there is nothing else which is exciting about it.

Further Control

Line the dog up to face the right hand dummy and give him the 'get over' command. This exercise should be exactly the same as those you have practiced on land with doubles, marks and distractions and therefore should be known by the dog. Any deviation off line towards the left hand dummy and you should try everything at your disposal in terms of verbal rebukes, commands and praise to keep your dog on track for the right-hand dummy and away from the diversion. As the dummies are well apart, this should be a simple task and also the right-hand one should be more attractive:

(a) Because it involves a long swim, and
(b) Because although initially quite interesting, the diversion made a splash but that's all!

Your diversion dummy thrower needs to be alert however and if necessary get the diversion out of the water either by grabbing it or pulling on the rope! Timing is crucial!

You should blow your stop whistle at the first sign of deviation and then give another right hand signal or a recall depending on which appears to be the most appropriate at the time.

If all goes well, with no real difficulties or only a small deviation, which was rectified, then try the same exercise with the 1st dummy on left and the diversion on the right.

If there has been a more difficult situation which has resulted in the dog being recalled and the diversion being hauled in by the dummy thrower set the exercise up again.

This time, throw the first dummy out into the water in exactly the same place as before. Then get the dummy thrower to throw the diversion on the rope, just onto the ground *towards* the water. In this way, hopefully, the dog will see the dummy you want as the most interesting! Try again to send the dog for the first dummy.

If that is successful, you should try again once or twice, with the diversionary dummy being thrown a little further each time and then try again but with both dummies on opposite sides. Make haste slowly!

It is important that you and the dog face both dummies, turning as appropriate to mark the fall of each. Do not attempt to shield the dog from seeing the dummy you do not want him to retrieve. Neither should you say 'leave it' or any other similar word. Try and keep everything exactly the same as when you practiced similar exercises on land. Take your time to ensure the dog faces the correct way for every dummy thrown and for when you send him on the 'go back' to retrieve.

Further developments

Knowing that your dog will ignore diversions and come back to you or follow a simple command to retrieve a dummy when there is a distraction of another dummy, will indicate that you will be able to set up more complex situations, and in particular, that you can begin directing the dog in water. Depending on the areas of water you have, try some of the following:

- Send your dog on a 'get over', stop, and throw dummy to the left or right. Give a 'get on' when the dog is in the water. Vary this so that sometimes you send the dog immediately, sometimes recall first.
- Use a mark to the left but send the dog to a blind on the right first and then for the mark from your side on the bank.
- Try 2 blinds
- Use a mark and then send the dog back to the same place to pick a blind.
- Use several marks on a far bank and get dogs to retrieve blinds at a closer distance from reeds or on another bank.

Further Control

- Have a mark thrown into the water and then send the dog from your side, to retrieve a blind hidden in reeds or across the water onto a far bank.
- Start to involve one or more other handlers and dogs. One or more dogs should then sit off lead watching and waiting without any whining, running-in or any other obedience issues, whilst another dog is working. This is also another situation useful for hunting practice where several dogs can hunt reeds etc. at different places round a lake.
- Send your dog on a 'get over' with no dummy in the water, blow the stop whistle and then throw 2 dummies, one to the left and one to the right. Send the dog for one of these (vary the order) and then send the dog for the remaining one from your side on the bank or send another dog.

Whilst practicing, keep up the work on straight forward marks across water and further back from the water once over it. Make sure your dog will continue to cross the water on one command. Try to ensure that your dog learns that on marks you will not stop him. It is still his job to go quickly to a mark and he needs to trust that this remains the way he was taught, the way it has always been, the way it always will be *no matter what*......................

Do not be tempted ever, to send your dog in the direction of a seen, marked, dummy with the intention of stopping him and then sending him in another direction. Later, you may have to send your dog *towards* a marked bird with the intention of then sending him to the left or right for an unseen wounded bird *however;* you will know before hand that the intention will be to stop your dog. The crucial difference will be in the *way* you send your dog in the first place.

It would never be appropriate to send your dog, in these circumstances, on his 'name' command. The name command must continue to mean to the dog that he is to go straight for the mark and nothing is going to happen in terms of you stopping him from doing this. *Marks are for life.*

If you intend stopping your dog, even though he may have to go *partly* in the direction of a bird he has seen land, then you should make something happen, in between him seeing or hearing the dummy or bird, and you sending him on a 'go back'.

You can do this quite simply be waiting for a while, moving slightly, turn round, *anything* which will break the concentration of the dog, from the mark onto whatever his task will be instead. I would be inclined to move slightly and give the dog a 'heel' command as I do it. The dog may only have to move ½ an inch but it is sufficient to break his concentration and get him to focus on something else.

Then you should line him up and send him on a 'go back' command.

By doing this, and if you have been consistent in the use of both the 'name' command and the 'go back' command, the dog will already be thinking, and knowing, that he will not be going to retrieve the mark or the bird or the dummy he saw land. That particular one becomes either the diversion or will become the second to be retrieved and not the main focus of his attention when he is sent initially.

When sent, the dog will already know he is not going for the mark. He will already be thinking, *'what's going to happen?'* To have a dog mentally prepared for his *next* task even though he does not know *when* he will be required to start it, or *where* it is likely to be, or *what* it is likely to involve, is a huge advantage. It is a help on land but on water, which is frequently more exciting and involves many other distractions, it is of immense benefit.

Handlers therefore need to be aware of these advantages and not put any previously learned tasks in jeopardy by not playing their own part in the proceedings, according to the book! This *is* a double act but with

Further Control

the dog having much greater and superior skills in these circumstances! He also has far more difficulties in this environment than the handler who is safe and dry on the bank. So be aware of the work your dog can do for you; work which could not be accomplished by a human, but also appreciate the difficulties faced by the dog.

Above all, handlers must play their part to perfection!

Tiggy
(Photograph: Mary Ward)

CHAPTER THIRTEEN

Tansy
(Photograph: David Tomlinson)

Common problems - Prevention and Treatment

Throughout the life time of training a gundog, recognising a dog's qualities, and using the assets which a dog has, there will inevitably be areas that are not quite as good as one would wish and there may also be a few problems which emerge. Problems can emerge at any time, with any dog, in any situation and there probably is no dog on earth which has not had a problem of one sort or another, from a handler's perspective, at some time of their life.

However hard one tries therefore it is not really possibly to ensure that a problem will never emerge and if anyone ever tells me they have never had a problem with their dog I tend to think that this is because: either the handler hasn't noticed, hasn't recognised it as a problem with the potential to get worse; has not seen that what a dog may be doing or not doing actually is a problem; or that a problem has not emerged, *yet!*

Further Control

Some dogs seem to create problems almost from the start and then settle down. Other dogs have problems now and again and yet others may get a long way through training before a problem may emerge but every dog will have something at some time.

How long the problem goes on before something is done about it is largely up to a handler and whether they are prepared to deal with it. It also depends on a handler recognising the difference between a dog which has not yet learnt something totally, in which case it is important to go on teaching in the same way until the dog has learnt, and a behaviour which has the potential to get worse rather than improve with time.

It is extremely difficult to recognise, in ones own dog, a situation which will get worse and we are all, not necessarily guilty of this but nevertheless in danger of ignoring things which we should do something about.

This is because of the emotional involvement we have with our dogs and the rose-coloured spectacles syndrome comes into the situation. We see our dogs in a way that outsiders do not and do not see our dogs in the way outsiders *do*. It is therefore vital that we have someone else who can observe us, and our dog, from time to time and give an opinion which we may not be able to give ourselves.

This opinion should be given to us on a regular basis if attending classes or one-to-one sessions with an instructor but if this is not the case, because you train your dog yourself, then those who enter competitions will in fact be given an opinion by a judge or an assessor.

Usually this judgement will be based on a dog's performance but implicit in this is the ability of the handler too and this is often more pronounced when one gets into more advanced competition. Handlers must learn to handle their own dog to the best advantage and sometimes this does not happen.

Apart from these types of assessment one usually sees for oneself in, or after, a competition where marks were lost in a test or why one did not get very far in a Trial. I believe it to be very important that a handler scores themselves after any kind of assessment or competition and then compares their own marks with the actual marks given by judges.

If you do this, there may be a difference of a point or two but if you are reading your own performance and that of your dog accurately you should find that in general you are able to assess yourself reasonably accurately in comparison with judges. These are also useful occasions for you to see for yourself where an area may need a little tweaking, pruning or major surgery in the days following any assessment. This applies to both dogs and humans!

With experience as an instructor one begins to see aspects of a dog's behaviour, as well as aspects of a handler's behaviour, which alert one to a problem brewing. It is this early detection process which can prevent rather than cure but there are also things presented to one that are actual problems and prevention is therefore not an option at that point.

I am now going to explain a few problems which are the most commonly perceived by an instructor, or which handlers are aware of themselves and present to an instructor. I shall also show ways in which it may be possible to start on the medication for effective cure.

One should never start to believe that, because there may be a cure for something, it is not worth trying preventive methods. The longer a problem develops the longer, sometimes, the cure will take to begin to work. Frequently there will be recurring symptoms when you least expect or want them! You can rub some things out, erase them, delete

Further Control

them from the hard-drive but there will always be a little bit left, some remnant of what used to be there; like some small part of the root of a weed, and it may not take much for it to start growing again!

<u>Swapping dummies.</u>

It is not until one begins advanced training with a gundog that one may encounter, for the first time a dog which, presented with more than one dummy in fairly close proximity, will put one dummy down and pick up another.

Some dogs never do this no matter how many dummies they may come across but for others the first time they do this should indicate to the handler that something needs to be done about it. The dog should never again, after the first time, be put into a situation where this could occur until you have tried to address the issue.

An even better way, other than seeing it happen for the first time, is for a handler to be aware that it *could* happen and therefore take as many steps as possible to avoid the dog actually doing it. I do not mean by this, that one should never put the dog into the situation where more than one dummy is available. It is vital that your dog is given experience of this but also, that he is taught what to do about it – or what not to do about it! You should just be ready, at that split second, to read that your dog is likely to swap, and get a quick growl in, followed by a recall. In this way you read the dog *thinking* about swapping. The punishment, by growling, will then punish the dog for thinking about swapping and this is far more effective than punishing a dog *for* swapping.

<u>Prevention.</u>

The prevention option should occur the first time a dog is faced with a situation of there being two, or more, dummies available and for this to be effective:

- The handler must be aware that, *'this is the first time my dog has been sent away from me on a 'go back'/hunting exercise where there is more than one dummy out.'*
- The awareness needs to be translated into action in terms of how the exercise is to be handled and thoughts then should concern the handler being fairly close to where the dummies are or close to the dummy the dog is likely to come across once he has the first one in his mouth.
- Set up the exercise with these points in mind but also think about how you are going to deal with the situation; bearing in mind that you are going to try to prevent the dog picking another dummy after he has retrieved one. It is no good thinking you will deal with the situation *after* a dog has dropped one dummy and already picked up another because you would then be trying to cure rather than prevent.
- You have several tools at your disposal:

(1) The fast recall whistle.

This option should be your first choice and timing is crucial.

As soon as the dog has the dummy in his mouth, the handler should immediately use the fast recall whistle, followed by a growl if the dog does not show signs of thinking he must get back to you quickly. Another fast recall whistle should then be given after the growl.

All this has to be done with split-second timing. A lot of praise should also be given to the dog as soon as he shows you that he is thinking of returning with speed, with the first dummy. Do not wait until the dog has actually returned to give the praise. The praise should be given for the dog thinking about doing the correct thing and that should be sufficient for the dog to continue doing what he has thought.

Further Control

If that does not work i.e. the dog continues to go in any direction other than straight back to you then you should be ready with another option.

(2) The stop whistle.

You can use this option if you have already taught the dog to obey a stop whistle at distance. If you have not taught this, and/or the dog has not learnt to obey the command, then there is no point in trying although a verbal command of 'sit' may be an alternative.

The command should be used if the recall command is not obeyed and it is used, not to make the dog sit immediately as such, but in terms of keeping in communication with your dog and as a *'watch me I am going to tell you what to do'*. When the dog looks, the sit command should be repeated and the dog made to obey. He should then be left in a sit for a few seconds whilst you walk closer to the dog. His attention should be fully on you, at this point and then a fast recall whistle command can be given.

If the dog only hesitates, praise him and then give the 'sit' command again and insist that he does sit. You can then follow this by praise again, repeat the stop whistle command, to *'watch me, because I'm going to tell you what you must do'*, and then a fast recall command.

The important factor is to keep in communication with your dog and you do this by any reasonable means at your disposal.

Whilst the dog is focussed on you he cannot go to pick another dummy, and it is for this reason you should also be making your way towards your dog. This approach should not be in a threatening way, but simply because by being closer, you can reinforce the recall command more effectively. You must insist the dog obeys the recall whistle so repeat any commands of stop whistle or recall with either a growl or praise according to the reaction of the dog.

If the dog does not pay attention to the stop whistle then you should have the next option up your sleeve!

(3) Your voice commands in terms of 'no' or 'leave it'. Either of these verbal commands may be appropriate, depending on whether either has already been learnt by the dog. Another useful verbal tool is *'Oy, what are you doing?'* said in a gruff voice.

So if your dog continues to go in any direction other than back to you and he ignores a stop whistle and recall and ignores you on anything else you have done, then shout whatever words you feel appropriate, other than a command word and also walk nearer to the dog so that you get his attention. If at any point the dog focuses on you he should immediately be praised and then a recall command given either verbally or with the whistle. If this recall command appears an unlikely option at the time, then a sit command may be preferable as too may simply to go to the dog and take the dummy from him – gently, and with appropriate praise.

With a dog from which you have had to take a dummy, make sure you keep control of the dog. There is no point at this stage, of taking the dummy from him and then just letting him go off and pick up the dummy you have spent all the time preventing him from picking up!

Sit him up in the same place and give him the dummy which you have just taken from him, with a *'hold'* command. Praise him and then move just a pace or two in front of him whilst reminding him to *'sit'* and *'hold'* with lots of praise. Then recall him with appropriate praise, present and more praise.

There are those who feel one should never use a stop whistle when a dog has a dummy in his mouth because that will interfere with the dog's thinking that he has to return to the handler quickly, immediately he has something in his mouth.

Further Control

I agree with that philosophy however, I believe you have to keep in mind the particular lesson you are trying to teach the dog. In this situation you are teaching *'you must not swap dummies'*; and reinforcing the fast recall concerning *'when you have something in your mouth, your job is to bring it back to me immediately'*. You are also dealing with a situation for which you are trying to prevent a more serious problem occurring, in circumstances which have not been experienced by the dog before.

The commands are the same but the circumstances are different. You are also reinforcing this by saying (a) *'no matter what else happens, no matter what else may be out there, your job remains that of bringing the dummy you have in your mouth back to me'* and (b) *'if you don't do that, I am going to do something about it in order to teach you that your job is the same in these circumstances'*.

Obviously you would not use a stop whistle in circumstances which were normal; in that your dog went out, found a dummy and was coming straight back to you with it. On this particular lesson however these are not normal circumstances, in that they have not, up to this point been experienced by the dog and therefore have not yet become normal and routine. I have never yet found a dog, when he has been stopped and then recalled in this way, which had a problem later, or even hesitated on return with a dummy. This is because if the above methods work, the dog will not need, in future, ever to be stopped in this way again and it will quickly disappear from his memory.

No dog *knows* that he should only bring one dummy or bird back at a time or that he should not put down one bird in favour of retrieving another, unless he is taught that this is what his handler wants.

The situation is such that if left to make this decision on his own, a dog may well try and bring back as many birds and dummies as he can fit into his mouth - and some have thoughts concerning this which grossly exceed the true capacity of their mouth! Or he may choose to swap if he comes across something which may appear to be a better choice. By his reckoning, if you are pleased with one dummy or bird being retrieved, you are bound to be 6 times as ecstatic by 2 or 3 being retrieved or a better one being retrieved!

The dog does not do this deliberately to upset his handler, which is how many handlers view the situation until they stop and think, or have it pointed out to them, that this has to be taught to the dog along with many other facts.

The above points are solely of use in a preventative situation and these should be borne in mind throughout any training exercise you attempt with the dog.

I should mention here that you should be careful concerning your praise in certain situations. I have had handlers who are absolutely ready to deal with preventing a dog picking up a second dummy after the first but the handlers forget one crucial aspect. That is that *'dogs point with their eyes'*. If the dog has one dummy in his mouth, hesitates and looks at a second dummy, the last thing a handler should do is say, *'good boy'*. Praise at that point would indicate to the dog that he is right in thinking he should pick up the dummy he is looking at!

If a situation has been allowed to develop, to the degree that the dog has already put down one or several dummies in favour of picking up another, then the following exercise may help. It has proved effective even with dogs which have a long history of this particular problem.

The cure.

One must keep in mind that however many times a dog may have swapped dummies, whether it is once or several dozen times that the dog is not being disobedient or deliberately setting out to be difficult. He is simply doing it because no-one has said he should not! The problem lies with the handler and not the dog and as such, handlers

Further Control

need to accept their own responsibility in this and not start teaching whilst believing it is the dog which is difficult.

This exercise is best attempted when you have an assistant, although it is possible to do it on your own. Take with you a toy or something you know your dog likes, this could be an old sock with a knot tied in the middle, which your dog loved whilst practicing 'holds' or anything of yours which you know the dog will want.

Keep the toy/sock hidden in your pocket. Next, arrange a large pile of dummies to create a substantial mountain – at least 6 dummies but preferably more! Let your dog see you doing this as there is no reason why he should not observe, although put him on a sit at a distance whilst you are creating the structure. Give the toy to your assistant and then take up a position about six feet away from the dummy pile with your dog at heel on a sit.

The chances are your dog will be totally focussed on this pile having watched, and wondered, what it was all about. Get your assistant to say 'mark', and place the toy on top of the dummy pile (See picture (a) below)

(a) The toy is placed on a pile of dummies.

Wait until your assistant gets out of the way and then send your dog on a 'go back'. As the dog is leaving your side you must take some steps forward so that you follow the dog and then give him a 'hold' command and encourage him to pick up the toy. As soon as he has it in his mouth you must praise him in a very exciting way and immediately say 'come'. At this point, turn your back and run away.

Hopefully your dog will run back to you thoroughly enjoying the new game! When he approaches you, turn round to face him, get down on the ground and make a bit fuss of the dog. You should not make any attempt to take the toy from the dog to start with but just praise the dog for a while, then stand up, put the dog on a sit and take the toy in the usual way.

Timing is crucial in the initial stages of this exercise, so you must make sure you give the 'hold' command when he is focussed on the toy, praise immediately he has the toy and then give the 'come' command instantly before rushing off in the opposite direction.

If you try this on your own, without assistance, you will have to leave your dog on a sit, go and place the toy and then return to the dog before giving the 'go back' command.

After the dog has retrieved the toy and brought it back to you, you can try the next part of the exercise.

Next, reduce the number of dummies and spread the pile of dummies out a little so that they are in a circle on the ground. They should all be touching each other but in a single story not a high-rise block. You therefore create a shallow table of dummies. (See picture (b)).

Further Control

(b) The toy is placed on a shallow table of dummies.

Stand close to the pile of dummies and again have the toy placed on top of them with a 'mark'. Follow the same procedure as last time by following the dog after you have sent him and give all the same commands with praise for obeying and then the final running away.

Next, reduce the number of dummies and spread them further apart so that there are spaces through which the dog has to tread. (See picture (c) below).

(c) The toy placed in the centre of spread dummies.

You must follow exactly the same procedure as before. You therefore keep most of the circumstances and the same commands each time, but the toy is placed slightly differently, in relation to the dummies, on each occasion.

Once these three steps have been accomplished, do not be tempted to do more. Let the dog think about it for a couple of days and then you will be ready to progress a little further.

On the next session start in exactly the same way as your previous session. Stand as before about six feet away and do everything the same as before except you should not follow the dog. You must use all the commands as before, and the praise, but stay where you are both after sending the dog and for the dog returning with the toy. The praise must be totally over the top for the dog when he achieves all this.

You should do the same three progressions in terms of the number and position of the dummies and where the toy is placed. In this way everything about the training should be what the dog knows from last time, with only one new thing changed. The change is that you will not follow the dog but will remain in position throughout.

If all has gone well, one more step can be added and that is to increase the number of dummies. Place the toy in the middle again but the dog will have to pass over and through many more dummies to retrieve the toy. (See picture (d))

If all goes well, leave the situation alone for a day or two and then have another session, building up very slowly but staying close to the first dummy so you can continue to give on the spot commands as needed. Aim to send the dog further and further, crossing over dummies, but with you remaining close to the first.

Use the toy throughout the first few sessions then you can begin again with a marked dummy.

Further Control

(d) Toy is placed within more dummies.

(Photographs: Anthea Lawrence)

When you first try with a dummy, go back to having a pile of dummies and place the marked dummy on top of the pile.

At this stage it is not important for the dog to retrieve the dummy which has been placed or thrown onto the pile; some dogs do and some do not. You should however, follow the dog up and be ready with a 'hold' command when the dog picks up a dummy (any one will do).

As soon as the dog has a dummy in his mouth you must praise and then give a quick recall. Be careful to praise when your dog is still looking downwards and has picked up the dummy. If you leave the praise too late, he may already be looking at another!

Build up gradually, as with the toy, spreading dummies out and working up to the point where you remain in position after you have sent the dog, for the recall and present.

Another aspect to incorporate at this time, but on a different session is to give the dog a straight forward marked retrieve with a dummy.

Whilst the dog is going out for the marked retrieve have two or three dummies placed on the ground close to you so that the dog has to cross these on his return with the retrieved dummy. You must be ready to insist that the dog does not deviate from the recall however.

This can later be developed into having a dummy thrown onto the ground to the side of the returning dog after he has retrieved. You must make sure that although he may hesitate and watch the fall of this dummy, he continues his return to you almost immediately.

After all this, you should be able to have several dummies scattered on a field, throw a dummy somewhere in the middle of these, and then send the dog to retrieve. It does not matter which dummy the dog retrieves. What matters, is that when he picks up the first one, that you are onto the recall whistle immediately so that he knows he must not deviate.

Anticipating on directional commands.

I mentioned in Chapter Nine that some dogs, and they tend to be the more outgoing, bold dogs, can anticipate which way they will be sent after they have been stopped. They may then start to move before given the command.

Handlers should always use the correct hand and arm, in conjunction with a stop whistle, if they know they are then going to send a dog in a certain direction i.e. if the dog is to be sent to the left of the handler then the left hand and arm should be used with the stop whistle. This then gives dogs a clue as to which way they will be sent next.

Further Control

This help is very useful for most dogs because although they won't move from the spot, once they have been stopped, they are beginning to anticipate *in their thinking*, which way they will be sent. The crucial aspect is, of course, that the dog does not move until sent.

Dogs are very good at picking up these signals and cues and if this is combined with a dog which is over keen to get on with the task, their thinking can go beyond thinking! A dog may start taking these cues as his command to go in that direction: either without stopping; or before waiting for the next command which will tell him precisely which way to go. i.e. forward left, directly left, slightly back and left etc.

Although many dogs will actually find the dummy and their guess will be accurate, one should not allow the dog to dictate either the pace or the direction, otherwise the situation may only worsen.

Handlers need to be aware of this happening and the first thing to do is calm everything down and make the dog wait. Often the opposite happens in that many handlers start getting quicker and quicker with their commands.

The handlers do this to keep up with their dogs!

This of course is the wrong message to give to a dog and actually encourages the dog more and more, to do precisely what he wants and that could mean less and less of what the handler wants. This can then lead to a dog which is basically out of control or beyond the control of its handler under certain conditions. One sees eventually, handlers giving commands to the dog *after* the dog has made the decision to go!

If you have noticed, or someone else has noticed that your dog anticipates, then goes beyond anticipation and actually moves before you give the subsequent command after the stop whistle, there are numerous techniques which you can try.

- Wind. Take careful note of the wind direction and set up exercises whereby the dog is not being fed the delights of scent coming from a dummy at the point where you stop him. This cuts out one of the motivating factors which could lead to a dog thinking for himself and anticipating your command.

This aspect of wind and scent also works in the opposite way when needed. If you have a dog which is hesitant about moving after a stop whistle for example, then use the wind and scent. Stop the dog precisely where strong scent is coming off a dummy or, better still, some cold game. Hesitant dogs will then be more motivated to go where you want, with the strong motivating scents.

Back to the *'eager beavers'* however!

- Use the wrong hand.

I know that I always say *'be honest with your dog'* and *'it's important to use the correct hand every time'*. I stick by these principles in terms of training and working a dog, as I believe this to be essential.

In these circumstances however, you are not training so much as re-training. You already have a problem, and sometimes the solution is simply one of making the dog calm down at a distance, re-focus on the handler and just wait until told where to go, and what to do.

For this reason, and only when the situation warrants it I would suggest using the opposite hand, together with the stop whistle, from the one which should be used.

For example; the dog is sent out on a 'go back' then stopped with the whistle and a left hand signal. Once the dog focuses on the handler the left hand should be dropped but the dog should be kept in a sit position for 30 seconds. These 30 seconds are terribly hard for a handler! The time should be used in praising the dog and repeating the

Further Control

sit command, by using the whistle and left hand signal high in the air above the head. This repeating of the sit command and the praise is in the same way as at the start of basic training.

After the 30 seconds, the left hand should be put down, the right hand raised, together with another stop whistle. Give two or three reminder commands of 'sit' with the stop whistle and right hand. Provided the dog remains in position, without moving then calmly give him a right-handed 'get on' command.

If the dog moves, at any stage before being given the 'get on' command then you should keep the dog sitting, by use of the whistle and left hand commands as before. Aim to keep him waiting a few seconds longer, every time he moves. You want him to learn that if he moves the situation becomes worse for him in that there is more delay before he is allowed to do what he wants to do.

When setting this up with handlers and dogs, I have found that the dogs learn this lesson very quickly. Unfortunately many handlers do not!

The problem for handlers is that they sometimes have no patience and cannot bear to wait! Waiting is absolutely crucial on this type of retraining so if you think you are the impatient type; take someone with you, who can hold you back!

It is important for the wrong hand, in these circumstances, to be used when setting up a variety of similar situations so that the dog is simply calmed down and learns the importance of watching and listening to the handler. Then, you should go back to using the correct hand on set exercises but continue keeping the dog waiting. It is perhaps the waiting which does the most good because frequently it is the handler who has been in too much of a hurry and responded to the dog's time-scale rather than getting the dog to accept the handler's time-scale.

I have found that this type of situation escalates because often handlers send their dog quicker and quicker because they think the dog will run-in. They therefore pre-empt the running-in by giving, what is in reality, permission to run-in. The dogs then stop waiting even for the permission to run-in and just go!

Tansy
(Photograph: David Tomlinson)

Further Control

CHAPTER FOURTEEN

Lily
(Photograph: Paul Lawrence)

Have your foundations started to crumble?

Sometimes, one can get so involved in advanced training; expecting the dog to do more and more, that some of the basic commands - those taught and learnt a year or so back, start to become less than reliable. This is not, usually, due to problem dogs!

Some of the signs to look for, which may indicate crumbling foundations are as follows: a dog may start pushing, just a little, but particularly in relation to the 'heel' and 'sit' commands in certain situations. By this I mean that you may find your dog is slightly ahead of you when supposed to be walking to heel. You may notice this particularly when doing a walk-up at a test, with a walking gun on a shoot, a walked-up Field Trial or any situation where the dog knows what is likely to happen.

This knowing is always on occasions where the dog is looking for something good to happen for him! He therefore pushes ahead, may sit, but always just ahead of you and certainly not in the position in which he should be.

On other occasions he may start to get up from a sit position when you are lining him up for a 'go back' or perhaps not waiting until you have finished the command before he is off!

These are not huge problems and many handlers ignore them because the dog is basically steady, may not run-in, is good at finding the bird or dummy and the handler sees the dog as *'oh, he's really keen, knows what to do almost before I tell him'*. What I see sometimes is a dog which is actually doing some things, before he is told.

When I see a few of these minor problems, I see a dog who is possibly in adolescence or just coming up to full maturity but more importantly, one who has begun to think *'I'm in charge now'* or has maybe just tried to *'improve'* things, from his point of view! His thinking along these lines is partly to do with enjoying his life as a gundog and all the outings he has. Mainly however, his thinking has developed because his handler has allowed a few minor problems to remain instead of letting the dog know, the first time he started thinking along such lines, that *'no, you can't redefine all these things'*. Commands are for life!

For many dogs which show these symptoms, they are not problem dogs as such and many of them will, in fact, push no further than they have already pushed at the time I or others notice it, but one never knows! If I have taught that a certain command means a specific action or position then I believe that should not change in relation to the basic 'heel', 'sit' and recall commands, ever. The command and the definition of the command must remain the same for ever,

That means vigilance on the part of a handler however and many dogs will test out whether a handler *really* means them to walk in a certain position or whether they *have* to put their bottom on the ground every time the 'sit' command is given.

Further Control

If a dog is testing this out *'just to see'* and a handler does not notice, or notices but does nothing about it, then the dog may well take this non-intervention to mean he can continue with his preferred interpretation.

You can guarantee that the preferred variety will be to the perceived advantage of the dog and not to the handler!

If the handler reacts to such a situation sometimes, but not always, there will be more attempts by the dog to change the basic command meaning. The dog will never stop pushing because sometimes it is allowed (non-intervention) and sometimes it is not allowed (intervention). The dog therefore is the position of *'heads I win, tails I may not win - but I may win next time'*. A true gambler!

👊 The pushers.

I believe these minor problems are better to be dealt with as soon as they are seen but if they have gone on for quite a while then a little remedial work may be necessary. First though, you must re-define, for yourself exactly what you want a command to mean and then insist that is what the dog must do, *come what may, no questions asked, no matter what........,* which is how it should have been from the beginning!

Make sure your dog continues to walk in the correct position, always. If the dog has started to stray a little when you are walking, put the lead back on and make sure the dog understands that the position has not changed. If you think you may have allowed the dog to believe it had changed, then it may take longer because you will now be teaching *'I allowed it to change, but now It's going back to how it used to be. I am restoring it to its former glory!'* Handlers must also believe they have the right to do this!

When beginning an exercise, you should not start until the dog takes up the correct positions as commanded. Some dogs start creeping forward of the handler or they sit sideways or they half sit or numerous variations on the exact position required. Handlers often disregard such things because they begin to think only about the exercise or are too desperate to send the dog to retrieve, particularly when the dog starts getting anxious to retrieve too.

It is much better simply to wait and let the dog figure out that until, and unless, he gets himself into the correct position, that nothing will happen.

Handlers must do this in a very calm manner however and take on the attitude of *'I've got all day, I can wait for ever on this'*. Handlers must also stand still! It is the dog's responsibility to get himself in the correct position in relation to his handler and not the other way round. Many handlers start to get into a situation where the dog decides where he will sit and the handler then gets into the dog's heel position.

This is the wrong way round! It is quite amusing at times to see dogs doing this. They sit, and then look over their right shoulder indicating to the handler to catch up and get themselves into the right place! Usually such dogs are not difficult dogs but simply those which have not been taught *'well, actually lad, it's me who is the Royalty in this partnership not you!'*

Handlers are obeying the dog's commands in this way and it is often glaringly obvious in a walk-up situation. A shot is fired, a bird comes down or a dummy is thrown and the dog goes forward or out to the side and sits. The handler then takes a quick step forward or side-ways to be in the dog's heel position! This then becomes further confirmation to the dog that either he is in charge or the handler has re-defined the command position. Usually it is simply that the handler is just bending over backwards or sideways to accommodate the dog and not inconvenience the dog at all.

Sometimes heelwork can begin to disintegrate too when just walking. Dogs may simply walk in a position, all the time, which is half a pace in

Further Control

front of the handler; again, not a huge problem but one which should be addressed.

I believe work on the lead is probably the best place to start for dogs walking or stepping forward of their handler. I know some people advocate the use of a stick to swing in front of the dog's nose when walking along but I have never found this satisfactory. The dogs dodge round it, and therefore are still out in front; or start walking further out to the left beyond the range of the swaying stick; or some start lagging behind. Others do it properly when you have the swinging stick but, they are not stupid, and revert to walking wherever they like, when the swinging stick is not present.

It may be worth trying to see if it works with your dog but I prefer to go back to teaching on the lead.

Put the lead on the dog and do some heelwork in a similar fashion to when you taught the dog when he was much younger except you should use a short lead in your left hand and keep the dog in the correct heel position. You can be fairly brisk in your walking and you should give no warning to the dog when you change direction. When you halt, say nothing; put your left hand which is holding the lead, down low towards the dog's spine, and simply exert some gentle pressure on the lead in a backwards direction.

This pressure should be gradually increased by your left hand moving backwards until the dog is correctly in position, at which time the lead should be slackened and the dog praised. You should then give a 'sit' command and insist that the dog sits in the exact the heel position and praise him when he does.

Keeping the lead short will guarantee that the dog feels the pressure before you dislocate your arm! You must be careful however to exert only gently pressure and this must be back towards the correct heel position and never in an upwards direction. Your arm will therefore be fully outstretched behind you.

Once the dog is beginning to get the message about this, then you need to exaggerate the situation, even if he is no longer in an incorrect position.

You do this by doing some heelwork, again on a fairly short lead and when you halt, stop by taking a step backwards. Again, you should say nothing to the dog but exert some pressure on the lead backwards, until the dog is in the correct place, when you must relax the lead and praise him. Once the dog understands he needs to correct himself, you will probably find your dog may start first of all to jump backwards into the heel position. Then he will begin to watch you more closely so that when you step back instead of just stopping, the dog stays with you and in fact walks backwards into a halt. Then you will hopefully find that he watches you more closely and stays in the correct position.

When you see this, then you can do some heelwork off the lead. All should be well, but watch out for any pushing forward. Nip it in the bud! Put the lead back on the dog immediately and repeat the remedial treatment before trying off lead again.

The above system seems to work for many dogs, but for some it does not!

If you find that despite the remedial work your dog still pushes ahead when off lead the following may help.

Set up a walk-up situation with preferably 2 or 3 other handlers and dogs. As soon as your dog is ahead of you (by one inch), either when walking or when you come to a halt, simply put the lead on him. Without saying a word, take him back from the line a few paces. Give him a 'sit' command, leave him there and you rejoin the line.

Further Control

You and the rest of the line should then walk forward a short distance, fire a shot and throw a dummy or just throw a dummy and send one of the dogs to retrieve. Whilst this is going on, you should turn round and face your dog behind the line and remind him that he is to continue sitting.

When the dummy has been retrieved, turn away, and then give your dog a 'heel' command and allow him to join the line with you again. Make sure he adopts the required heel position and give him a 'sit' command. When everything is correct you, your dog and the line can begin walking-up again.

You must be prepared to go through the above sequence for as many times as it takes for the dog to learn that as soon as he is in the wrong place things get worse for him. You therefore need to make things increasingly worse for him by moving him back from the line further and further on each occasion you have to do it.

You repeat this for as long as it takes the dog to remain in the correct position when he joins the line. At that point your dog should have the next retrieve.

Having had the retrieve however is the time when the dog may revert to previous behaviour. You must be prepared for this and immediately revert to taking him away from the line again. Usually this is just a one off by this stage as it is only the dog checking if you really mean it. You must not fail this test however by allowing the dog to take up anything other than the correct position. Your dog must never believe he can have his reward – a retrieve, and then do as he likes. You must immediately take him on the lead, a long way back, to remind him.

Most dogs get the message! It also makes sense for them to be with the pack and obey the leader's commands!

🐾 The Laggers.

For lagging, lead work may help but frequently those who lag behind, have the correct heel position on the lead and revert to lagging again when off the lead. These dogs are often sensitive and may lack confidence when off the lead.

I have tried numerous ways to cure lagging and few worked very well because I used to try and also get a handler to try and encourage a dog to keep up. I then realised, what I should have realised before, and that is that pushing and lagging are the same problem just with different symptoms.

The problem is that the dog is not obeying the heel command. Once I understood this, then I stopped the encouraging – almost begging really! I had been taken in, as we so often are, by dogs which were sensitive! Whatever the type or personality of the dog, commands must be obeyed, *'no matter what…………………'*

Once I realised that it was the same problem as the pushy dogs then, of course I realised that the solution was the same too. So the walk-up setting is again the best to set up in order to address the problem.

Up to this point, if your dog has a lagging problem, you have probably been talking, encouraging, tapping your leg, doing everything you can think of, to keep the dog with you and it hasn't worked!

If it has not solved the problem, this is because all these things you have been doing have been viewed by the dog as almost praise. By keeping up a conversation in a pleasant voice and keeping the dog feeling reasonably comfortable in its position behind you, it has been saying to the dog *'it's all right for you to be there, I know it's scary for you, but I am going to make you as comfortable as possible in the position you want to be in'*. It is also saying *'I have re-defined the heel position, and it's all right for you to walk there'*.

Further Control

The lagging needs to be exaggerated, which is the opposite of how one would believe it should be! Also the comforting factors, when the dog is in the wrong place, need to be removed. This is done by walking-up in the normal manner. Give one 'heel' command to the dog and then ignore him. This means *totally!* So you should not say anything to him; you should not do anything other than give the 'heel' command *once* then walk. Most importantly, you should not look at the dog. Dogs point with their eyes and they also check out this aspect in their handler. So if the handler looks where they want the dog or looks where they are going in this case, this works the best.

You must adopt the feeling of '*I am going in this direction. I want you to come too but I am not going to beg you, so you must please yourself*'. In that way you will not be conveying signs to the dog, in your body language, that you really, *really*, want the dog to come with you or that you are going to do everything you can to plead! You should no longer beg the dog to come with you! After a few paces, if your dog is lagging behind, simply stop the line, and return to your dog. Go into the heel position of the dog, give him a 'sit' command and make the dog remain in a sit where he has decided to be.

Leave the dog and then you should rejoin the line whilst the line moves forward thus creating a larger and larger gap between the dog and the line (the rest of the pack). Usually this type of dog will remain in position but if necessary, give reminder 'sit' commands and after a while, when the line halts, return to the dog, put the lead on and return to the line with the dog. Make sure the dog is in the correct heel position and praise thus showing the dog '*this is what I want you to do, this is where I want you to be*'. You should then give a 'sit' command, followed by praise, before removing the lead.

Give the dog the chance to stay with you at heel again when the line moves on but you must follow the same policy of one 'heel' command, walk and don't look at the dog. At the first sign of lagging, repeat the action of leaving the dog behind the line on a sit.

This time, wait so that the distance between the dog and the line is a little greater before returning to the dog. Some dogs figure this out very quickly and keep up after only one or two attempts. Others take a little longer because they are convinced that their handler will start the pleading, and any other inappropriate behaviour, again. Handlers should not stop this particular remedial exercise until the dog has learnt to keep up with the handler, otherwise it will take longer next time it is tried.

It doesn't make much difference whether dummies are thrown, shots are fired or your dog sees another dog retrieving because that is not usually the issue with these types of dogs. However all these things can be done with the other dogs in line provided you keep in mind what you are trying to achieve with your dog.

Similar techniques can be used for dogs which won't move off a sit when given a 'heel' command. Again, these are not truly difficult dogs but handlers should stop begging the dog to do it. It works much better to give one 'heel' command and then just go! Handlers must be careful not to turn round and look at the dog! The greatest problem is usually that handlers have got into many rituals of persuading the dog to come with them. The dog has therefore started to believe that all these steps are part of the command. They don't get themselves up until everything has been done and said in exactly the right order – oh, and nicely, because these dogs get a bit upset and huffy if anyone talks to them in less than deferential terms! (See *Respect & Leadership in dog training & related articles*')

Getting a handler to say 'heel' in a normal voice and then just to walk, without turning round, and sometimes disappearing out of sight, is quite difficult. This is why, in basic training, one should never start to do anything other than ensure the dog understands that one command means a certain action. Handlers who have different commands to the dog for every time the handler changes direction, frequently have the

Further Control

greatest problems in this. The 'heel' command, or whatever command a handler uses for the 'heel' position, should be the only command needed. It does not matter in which direction a handler goes; the position remains the same for the dog.

Handlers do not like to break habits which have been growing in number, over certain issues, for months and sometimes years. They are also usually very charming, pleasant people who feel they have been trying to do the right thing. Such handlers are never rough with their dogs but they are not tough enough or prepared, sometimes, to pretend to be tough and stop being over pleasant. Once the handler is able to do this however, the dog grasps the changes very rapidly and comes to no harm because of it.

If the dog is given the choice of (a) walking with the handler when he hears the 'heel' command and then being praised or (b) being left behind where he gets no sympathetic looks, pats, pleading and company, he opts for (a).

That is a surprise to most handlers! The reason for this is that handlers think they have been doing everything to help the dog, and cannot fathom why the dog is still having trouble coping. The handler then believes, if the helping props are removed, the dog will be able to do even less!

It works the other way round and usually works after three or four attempts! It works because the dog's pack instincts tell him he should remain with the pack. The handler's instincts were over-ruling this in thinking *'my poor dog needs so much help on this and I will do whatever I can to help him.'*

There are many instincts of a dog which we do not allow to have full reign. There are other instincts which we take control of and utilize in part and yet more that we should channel and make use of in their entirety. Pack instincts are the ones which we should use but we need to understand them before being able to do this. Reading about pack instincts can be really helpful in understanding and reading your dog.

👁 Dogs going the wrong way.

This can be on anything really but the most frequently seen are:

<u>On a mark where the dog does not go straight to the fall.</u>

These dogs need to be viewed as two distinct groups as different solutions apply according to the type of dog and therefore the type of problem it is likely to be.

👁 Those which simply do not mark very well.

If the dog does not go straight to the fall, he should be recalled immediately and the dummy then thrown again, and again and as many times as it takes, in exactly the same place in exactly the same way. Do not be tempted to handle the dog. His job is to watch and then go immediately to the area.

I believe that handlers can create bad marking dogs or make poor markers even worse.

The rules for a mark should be that the word 'mark' is said once only by whoever is throwing the dummy. Both handler and dog should keep their eyes forward and on the dummy from start to finish – from 'mark' to the fall. The handler should then say one word, the dog's name, and the dog should go accurately to retrieve the dummy.

Dogs described as bad markers frequently look, not at the dummy, but at their handler and usually handlers have created this by one or more of the following:

i. The handler saying 'mark'.

Further Control

ii. Putting a hand up in the air or pointing towards the dummy.
iii. Looking down at the dog instead of looking, all the time, at the dummy.
iv. Throwing too many marks themselves from their side.
v. Allowing dummy throwers to say 'mark' several times in an attempt to get the dog looking at them.

If any of the above is happening, you need to stop any or all of them immediately. Then you should start to re-train the dog on the rules of a marked retrieve as above and never, ever, do anything else.

Start with a very close mark and build up very gradually making sure that you do none of the above and if the dog does not go immediately, the dummy should be picked up and you start again. It will work if you persevere.

🐾 Those which actually enjoy hunting more than finding.

These dogs are immediately noticed because they are hunting all the way out towards the dummy or they hunt frantically near where the dummy is, or in larger areas surrounding the dummy. Some even blink the dummy in favour of hunting and often only retrieve it as a last resort. If you have a hunting dog of this type there is no point in recalling the dog and doing the exercise over and over again because this simply gives the dog more opportunity to hunt and still does not teach him to go straight to the fall.

Some dogs, find out very quickly that *'if I do it incorrectly, I get recalled and then I get several more opportunities to hunt'*. Re-calling the dog and having the dummy thrown again, as above for poor markers, will therefore make the problem worse. In this case you should try a different approach if the dog does not go straight to the fall.

Recall the dog, then have the dummy thrown again and *send another dog to retrieve it*. If that's not possible then you must do this yourself. Having recalled the dog, have the dummy thrown, leave your dog in a sit and go and retrieve the dummy yourself.

Once the dummy has been retrieved, either by another dog or you going out and picking it up, then you should have the dummy thrown again. Send the first dog again – many will go straight to the dummy.

If not, repeat the whole sequence so that the non-marking dog never goes twice in succession when he has failed to mark or has failed to go straight to the dummy. Do not be tempted, ever, to handle any dog on a mark in training. You should also keep up the remedial treatment whenever you are training and never allow the dog to hunt, except in the correct place.

With dogs of this type you should make sure that the marks are in very unexciting places and, if you have to repeat the remedial treatment several times on each attempt, make it worse for the dog each time by making the mark *closer* each time. If the dog will not go straight for this type of mark then he should not be given the opportunity to go for more exciting, further away dummies until he has learnt what his job is!

<u>On a 'go back' either from the handler's side or at a distance.</u>

If the dog goes in the wrong direction, or sometimes the dog will not go far enough on one command, stop the dog *as soon as it goes wrong* and praise the dog for stopping. Recall the dog and the exercise should then be started again in exactly the same way. This should be done calmly and in exactly the same way as before, to allow the dog to learn what you want and what he should have done. If you change things, the dog cannot make sense of it!

No punishment, other than a growl if necessary, is needed. Stop everything, start again, have a dummy thrown again, do whatever you were doing in exactly the same way and the dog will learn.

Further Control

Most frequently, when a dog goes the wrong way immediately it is because a handler has then tried to handle the dog from where he is after going wrong. This is, in effect, saying to the dog that he is correct in going the wrong way, which is the wrong message. It is the initial going wrong which has to be stopped.

Going the wrong way has to be dealt with so that the dog can understand he *has* gone wrong and the only way that will happen, is if he is brought back immediately and everything starts again and again if necessary. The handler must be prepared to stop everything and start again just *one more time* than the dog is prepared to do it incorrectly!

🐾 Dogs moving when left in a certain position.

Sometimes when setting up exercises it is necessary to start with a dog at a distance. What can often happen in more advanced training is that dogs start creeping a bit when a handler is moving away or putting dummies out *or talking*. Dogs get up or lie down or do something fairly minor rather than do exactly what they have been commanded to do.

Some dogs creep a bit and then sit again but it is important for a handler not to allow the creeping and not allow the dog to decide where to sit or to decide to adopt any other position.

It is also important *not* to command a dog, in these circumstances, with any command, after the dog has moved and whilst the handler is at a distance. This particular aspect is very important and yet one sees it continuously. The handler sees that the dog has moved in some way and immediately blows the whistle and gives the 'sit' command from a distance. This means that the handler allows the initial movement by the dog and the dog will keep doing this because it is in effect saying to the dog that it is all right for him to do it.

The dog believes he is permitted to move, which he is not!

You should always punish an incorrect behaviour but then show the dog, by putting him back, what he should have done. If you allow a dog to move and then handle him from a distance by repeating a sit command, then he has got away with the first mistake. The dog will therefore take this to mean *'it's OK for me to move a bit closer'* or *'it's OK for me to stand or lie down even though I've been told to 'sit''*.

What you should do, is keep your eye on your dog and give him a reminder 'sit' command, with praise, every so often. This is much better than having to act *after* he has moved.

A handler should always keep half an eye on their dog whenever they are at a distance. Then if the dog moves either by getting up, or creeping or going from a sit to a down the handler should start walking back to the dog, growl, put the lead on and, in silence, take the dog back to where he was left originally. The lead should then be removed, an appropriate command given, the dog praised for obeying and the handler should then leave the dog again.

A handler may have to do this more than once if a dog has been allowed to get away with this previously. For persistent or long-term offenders, it is best to put them back on the same spot once only.

That means that the handler goes back to the dog, shows the dog what he should do, leaves the dog, but only allows the one mistake. If the dog moves again I find it best to take the dog back further each time, than he was previously, thus making the situation worse and worse for him each time he moves.

Most dogs soon figure it all out and realise things are getting worse for them the more they move! You must not give up however, even if it takes the whole of the training session and you cannot do anything else.

This type of problem should not be allowed to start and if handlers make a habit of continuing to practice a few basics every so often then

Further Control

this is an issue which can easily be remedied. The important aspect is that a dog should know that when left in this way he can relax as he is not required to do anything.

I think handlers can, inadvertently, encourage movement by a dog by recalling too frequently after a dog has been left. In *'Taking Control'* I mentioned that you should always go back to your dog more often than you recall him. This meant for life! Handlers get lazy and having left a dog, gone a distance away, looked at ground, put dummies out and generally set up a wonderful training exercise; they can't be bothered to go all the way back to get the dog – so the dog is recalled! This really is false economy of effort! It may make sense to a handler but in so doing, the dog is being encouraged to anticipate a recall. Having a dog able to be left in one place and a handler knowing the dog will not move *come what may,* could save a dog's life! You should never let a dog anticipate any command, but I would place a recall command as *the* most important command *not* to be anticipated under any circumstances.

....

None of these situations represent horrendous problems; seeing these aspects in your dog, does not mean you have a problem dog but means that little things can become big things. Mostly they are a way of your dog experimenting just to see if you mean it. Well, you have to show your dog that you *do* mean it!

Mostly basic commands are a means of simplifying life for you and your dog. Commands have one specific meaning. If you have taught your dog that *'sit, means sit, no matter what..................',* then the dog should be able to relax, secure in the knowledge that nothing will happen, which he needs to be part of unless, and until, you give him another command.

If you allow the dog to creep, push, lag or any slight re-defining of commands for himself, he can't relax because he will keep on pushing a bit more because his security has disappeared. Every time he has pushed against the goal posts they have moved!

This means that you too will not be able to relax because most of your concentration will have to be on watching the dog in case he moves or does the wrong thing.

In training it is frequently necessary to leave the dog whilst you check out areas of ground, put dummies out, or get over fences and styles.

Yes, I know it's a nuisance, having climbed over a style; you see your dog move and then have to climb back over the style to re-position him. But you are training, and as such, the little things are as, if not more, important than the spectacular retrieves you set up. So take that bit of time, make yourself do the annoying, tedious little things. They are not difficult to do they're just the 'boring, can't be bothered' bits to which on the whole, we are all guilty of turning a blind eye on occasions when it suits us.

To set things up properly: looking at ground, checking for any dangers, and putting dummies out means you need to concentrate on what you are doing. You do not want, always, to have the dog with you on these occasions and neither do you want to put the dog on a lead or tie it up – as some people have to do! We must always be aware and keep a watch on dogs however, when we have left them in this way. None of us can be 100% certain of our dogs but we can nearly reach that percentage if we practice and do not allow any slight deviation.

I think we should also be aware of our conversation with others when we are at a distance from our dog. Sometimes we get involved in discussion about an exercise and say words which are commands and often say dog's names. All legitimate conversation when we set up an exercise *but* if a dog hears one or more of those words and obeys them when he is at a distance from us, we may think he is being disobedient!

Further Control

We need to be careful!

So, regarding foundations, tackle the small areas of difficulty and they will no longer be small areas of difficulty - they will disappear.

If you do not tackle the small areas of difficulty, they will no longer be small areas of difficulty either – *they will turn into problems!*

So, a bit like having a 'Spring Clean' when you turn out cupboards and throw away rubbish you should have turfed-out a long time ago; have a clean up on your basics, re-point your foundations, take back the control you had in the beginning and see whether a bright shiny image suits you and the dog better!

Lily
(Photograph: Paul Lawrence)

CONCLUSION

Nuala
(Photograph: Sharon Rogers)

I hope that you have enjoyed reading *'Further Control'* and that some of the ideas concerning training have been useful to you in applying a bit of polish!

As with everything needing a polish it is the one applying the polish who has to work and apply the elbow grease.

Advanced training is no different!

I have written a lot about handlers and handling in *'Further Control'* and this is not because I am trying to have a go at handlers – despite what some of my pupils may feel!

In relation to dogs, I class myself firstly as a handler and I too have many difficulties and issues with my dogs and how I handle them. It is a never-ending cycle of vigilance, being aware of what is happening, monitoring oneself and reading the dog. Few of us can do this without help and if there are times when it sounds as though I am being 'picky', well this is true! It is paying attention to detail and I believe that little things mean a lot!

Further Control

Basic training should have sorted out any dog problems and if these have not been sorted out, then advanced training is not an option because neither dog nor handler will be ready.

Advanced training is, of course, concerned with training the dog as the primary focus. In the same way as driving a car however, if the driver has not perfected basic driving skills on the family saloon, going on to a top of the range, sporty model will not improve the driving skills. The driver would in fact become quite a hazard and liability on the roads.

I know dogs are not machines, but as with machines they do need an operator! The performance and resulting quality will depend more on the skills, knowledge and experience of the operator, the more sophisticated or advanced the desired end product becomes!

Apart from a variety of references to applying training to shooting situations, I have not specifically included a great deal of information about shoots and the variety of jobs for which dogs may be required. This is deliberate: firstly because the variety of jobs for dogs are so numerous, that each would require a separate book; secondly because whether a dog is ready to be taken on a shoot, will depend on so many factors.

The type of dog, whether it is physically and mentally mature, whether all the basic commands have been learnt and can be applied when needed; whether a handler has full control of the dog in all circumstances; will all have a bearing on whether the dog is ready.

Many dogs are taken on a shoot before they are ready, in my opinion, and often people are in too much of a hurry to get the dog out that they forget the above factors.

I feel that most dogs are not fully ready to do a whole day's shooting for the whole season, for several years. I have had dogs ready before they are two years old and others not ready for a year or two after this.

More dogs are ruined, by being taken too early, than are ever ruined by being taken a little later!

Shoot experience has to be gained by the dog and as with other facets of training, this takes as long as it takes for the dog to learn, and they are all different.

There is a lot of talk these days, concerning the use of cold game for training gundogs and the fact that many people feel this shows a lack of respect for the birds. My own view is that we must respect the fact that the shooting of game birds should always be with the intention for these to be used as food. They are birds for the table and this is the whole reason why gundogs must be controlled, need swiftly to locate and retrieve wounded birds and must retrieve tenderly to hand.

It is also the reason why handlers too must deal with all birds retrieved in a professional manner, which includes dispatching wounded birds speedily and in a way which tries to ensure that the bird is still fit for the table.

I personally do not like the thought of hoarding an enormous quantity of shot birds in the freezer which I would use simply to throw around to enable dogs to retrieve them and then throw them away. This is one of the reasons I am no longer in favour of Cold Game GWT's. I feel members of the general public have a right to be concerned if they witness dead birds being thrown in this way simply for dog competition purposes.

I do believe however, that young dogs need experience of picking up cold game: to learn about the scents emanating from a variety of birds as well as the different textures of feather in their mouths; and for handlers to ensure that the dog is not going to bite a bird, tear the feathers out or start to play with it. Of course this is slightly different in some aspects from how it may be with warm game and injured birds, but it is a start.

Further Control

Dogs must have this experience and I believe that for training purposes I have no other way of doing this unless it is by using cold game.

I see the use of cold game in a similar way to medical students having to work on cadavers when in training and do not see any viable alternative. The bird or human body has then to be treated with respect within the parameters of the circumstances.

I try, when I have a young dog, to introduce them to as many separate varieties of game bird as I can and therefore try to ensure my dog has picked up Pheasant, Duck, Wood Pigeon, Woodcock, and Partridge before going on a shoot.

Often these birds are available either as very young birds culled at the game farm or birds from the game cart which are unsuitable for the game dealer. Other times I have had to purchase a brace of birds when I will usually eat one, and use the other for training purposes.

I believe that this interim step between dummies and warm game to be an essential step for any dog. Every individual needs to have their own view of the situation however and I would not seek to tell people how to behave in relation to these aspects other than to say that I feel we have an obligation to be careful in these matters. It is a sad fact of the times that we are unable to train our gundogs in quite the same way as a few years ago.

Some of the differences are to the good, in terms of the way dogs are treated, but other aspects such as: not being able to use starting pistols, dummy launchers and the sound of a shot in certain places, having to be careful to hide ourselves away from public gaze if we are introducing a young dog to holding a dead Partridge, all make life a little complicated for us.

I believe we have to try, however resentful we feel about this at times, to accept the current sensitivity, of some people, to what we do even if we do not shoot birds ourselves. The future of shooting and country pursuits in general, depends on us all doing our best to change anything we can, without compromising our own interests. The future of breeding, owning and working our dogs depends on shooting. Without it, the future of all our dogs will be bleak; the so called gundogs of the future and their characteristics will not be those we know today and there may not be the opportunity of getting them back.

Concerning when a dog should experience a shoot, the age of a dog has some bearing on the situation as well as when the dog is born, in relation to the shooting season. If you have an older trained dog then introducing a youngster is considerably easier, as one can then take the young dog but still function in whatever capacity you are working.

If beating or picking-up we must remember that we are there to work for the keeper and shoot owner and are not there simply to train a dog. Look for opportunities however and if it is possible for you to take a young dog to a shoot without having a paid role, then use the opportunity. Alternatively some experienced beaters and pickers-up may be able to take you with them somewhere or you may be able to stand with a friend who is shooting on the day. All these people will be able to help in terms of the etiquette of shooting and what the dogs will be required to do as well as giving you opportunities to perhaps watch a drive, give your dog some retrieves and some hunting and sweeping up experience.

I can't tell you when your dog is ready to go on a shoot. I could only give an opinion about this if I knew you and your dog: witnessed the level of training achieved; as well as the level of control you have of your dog. If you are not sure, then find someone who can help you.

I said at the beginning of the book that this is a journey. It is also a mystery tour in some ways because with any dog one is never quite

Further Control

sure, at the beginning, where this journey will take you. You will have to explore pathways that will be new as well as pathways that may be familiar but you will have, hopefully, all learnt something new and seen things you may never have seen before.

I wish you all well. The journey is not over: it continues for the lifetime of the partnership between you and your dog. I hope you continue to enjoy it and collect many souvenirs along the way which will later become your memories.

Anthea Lawrence

Nuala
(Photograph: Sharon Rogers)

Also by Anthea Lawrence

Published in 2006   ISBN 1-4120-9942-0

Taking Control
Anthea Lawrence

The How & Why of Basic Gundog Training
(For any variety gundog)

Available from www.trafford.com and www.amazon.co.uk

Published in 2005 ISBN 1-41205478-8

Respect & Leadership in dog training
& related articles
Anthea Lawrence

Available from www.trafford.com

ISBN 1425159864-9